Teaching Literature
IN THE CONTEXT OF
Literacy Instruction

JOCELYN A. CHADWICK

JOHN E. GRASSIE

HEINEMANN
Portsmouth, NH

Heinemann
361 Hanover Street
Portsmouth, NH 03801–3912
www.heinemann.com

Offices and agents throughout the world

© 2016 by Jocelyn A. Chadwick and John E. Grassie

The authors and publisher wish to thank those who have generously given permission to reprint borrowed material:

Figures 2.1, 2.2, and 2.3 and text excerpts (1996) from the collection by Tim Rollins and K.O.S. Reprinted by permission of Lehmann Maupin Gallery.

Figure 3.2: Bill of Sale for Hannah (1828) from the private collection of Jocelyn A. Chadwick and John E. Grassie. All rights reserved.

Figure 3.3: Daniel Defoe's *Journal of the Plague Year* courtesy of Lilly Library, Indiana University, Bloomington, IN. Reprinted by permission.

Figure 3.3: Title page of *Memoirs of Samuel Pepys* (1825). Reprinted by permission of the Irvin Department of Rare Books and Special Collections, University of South Carolina.

Figure 3.5: Front page of *The Elevator* (June 21, 1867). Reprinted by permission of the American Antiquarian Society, Worcester, MA.

Excerpts from *Common Core: Paradigmatic Shifts* by Jocelyn A. Chadwick. Copyright © 2015 by Jocelyn A. Chadwick. Published by Cambridge Scholars Publishing. Reprinted by permission of the publisher.

Credits continue on page iv.

Cataloging-in-Publication Data is on file at the Library of Congress.
ISBN: 978-0-325-07474-0

Editor: Tobey Antao
Developmental editor: Alan Huisman
Production: Victoria Merecki
Cover design: Suzanne Heiser
Cover images: © Getty Images/221A (book spine); © Getty Images/WIN-Initiative (girl reading)
Interior design: Bernadette Skok
Typesetter: Valerie Levy, Drawing Board Studios
Manufacturing: Steve Bernier

Printed in the United States of America on acid-free paper

19 18 17 16 15 PPC 1 2 3 4 5

This book is dedicated to the legions of English teachers, past and present, whose efforts have helped students explore the adventures of literature, search the depth of the thoughts and new ideas expressed in books, and, finally, draw from the experience of reading, the foundation of literacy—a gift that shapes students' lives and their ability to express themselves forever.

Among the many dedicated teachers, I, Jocelyn, have known as a student and then in my career as an English teacher, two very special people stand out: Judith Ann Purvis and Patricia Taggart Munro. They were my mentors and patient counselors when I was a young teacher and have remained true friends, colleagues, and valuable collaborators ever since. In so many ways, this book would not have been possible without their thoughts, insights, and always well-reasoned contributions.

Thank you, Judi and Pat, you are and will always be my best thing.

Credits continued from page ii:

Figure 5.1a: Bill of Sale for Armsted (1858) from the private collection of Jocelyn A. Chadwick and John E. Grassie. All rights reserved.

Figure 5.1b: Paris Codex Image 09 from Northwestern University Library, http://digital.library.northwestern.edu /codex/codex.html.

I Care and Am Willing to Serve and Work to Protect All *Children* by Marian Wright Edelman. Copyright © 2014 by Marian Wright Edelman. Reprinted by permission of the Children's Defense Fund, Washington, DC.

$\mathcal{C}$ontents

foreword

We hope this book will help all of us who love literature to share it with students in a way that is meaningful, powerful, and useful to them, so that they can embrace it as their own. We consider literature a bridge to the kinds of skills that standards require, yes, but, more importantly, a bridge to a deeper understanding of the world. To begin this book, we asked our dear friend Hal Holbrook—a man whose love of reading has helped to shape the world's understanding of some of the central works of American literature—to share his journey as a reader and as a human being.

Books can open the world up. Steinbeck's *The Grapes of Wrath* taught me about hope lost in the dust storms of the '30s and people looking for it in the fruit-picking farms of central California while starvation stared them in the face, and their fellow Americans went for them with clubs and guns because they didn't want them around. Never heard about that. Theodore Dreiser's *An American Tragedy* taught me about the loneliness of a young man like myself and his yearning for love. And *Huckleberry Finn* showed me how cruel people can be to each other and the spirit of kindness in a man whose color was black. I would never have found all those stories of true life without books.

Why did nobody ever read a book in my house? Was their mind made up? Actually I was raised by my grandfather in New England, me and my sisters, and Grandpa had firm notions about everything. He was our champ, we loved him, but his were the only opinions available. The first book I read was *The Will to Win*, one of the Rover Boy books. *Do or Dare* was next. Grandpa must have picked them out for me because there was nobody else around except our nurse. Mom and Dad had hit the open road when we were babies and they never came back, so it must have been Grandpa. That book, *The Will to Win*, may have defined my life.

But not quite. Somebody cast me as Hamlet in a class project, so I had to find out who he was and why he was so screwed up about his Mom. That tapped into my Mom who wasn't there and made me think dark thoughts about her. So Will Shakespeare opened up that door. When I left Boston on a World War II troop ship, I carried two books: the Bible for some closeness to God before I got shot at and *The Grapes of Wrath*. I bogged down in the "begat" section of Genesis, but John Steinbeck's book about the Dust Bowl Okies looking for a new life in the mythical heaven of California kept me from getting seasick below decks, down near the propeller and the stinking diesel fuel.

When President Truman dropped the bomb on Japan, that saved me from being massacred in an American invasion and maybe told me to do or dare harder when I got back to college. My grades improved; and then I stumbled across Mark Twain just when folks down South were lynching black people Saturday night and singing hymns on Sunday. *Huckleberry Finn* took note of that and it wasn't very funny. Neither was the country I was born and brought up in and neither was the world around me that *The Rover Boys* may have been lying about, along with an awful lot of people. Mark Twain used them for target practice.

Now I was the first one in the family to read books. Maybe my sisters did, in the middle of their pretty desperate lives, but I was going to make a living out of them. Mark Twain's. Because the truth I couldn't find in life or the Bible as it is reasoned out in churches, I could find in books by him and by people who wrote about Abe Lincoln and John Adams. They carved out the meaning of *Democracy*. I began to study them as I took on the character of Mark Twain and started making a living at it on the stage. Been at it now for sixty years. All started with reading *The Will to Win*.

In a world loaded with information at your fingertips on smart phones, "Why not go to Google?" a young person might ask. "Why waste time reading books?" There's the rub. Information by satellite is not knowledge. Being there is in the book. The deep immersion you get in a story, the feelings that surround you watching Teddy Roosevelt fighting the country's takeover by hugely powerful people in the world of the 1890s in *The Bully Pulpit*, that can give you the emotional experience of time travel to an earlier world. Then you get it. You are there. You get what Pink Floyd is saying in *The Wall*. You can compare it to *Now* and say "Have we learned anything?"

This book by Chadwick and Grassie is a kind of diving platform into the wider pool of knowledge our imagination can open up to us, and shows us the unknown mysteries we face every day: how other people think.

—Hal Holbrook

*a*cknowledgments

We thank each and every contributor listed below and the hundreds of students without whose insights and perspectives our book would indeed be the poorer.

Angela Baldwin	Logan Manning
Anne Ruggles Gere	Louann Reid
Carol Jago	Luis Rodriguez
Courtney Morgan	Marian Wright Edelman
Cynthia Christopherson	MaryCarmen Cruz
Daniel Bruno	Micayla Fisher (and parent)
David E. E. Sloane	Michael LoMonico
Emily Hamm	Neal Shapiro
Hal Gessner	Patricia Jones
Hal Holbrook	Patricia Taggart Munro
Holly E. Parker	Pedro Nogura
James Mulreany	Ramah (Rae) Troutman
Janis Mottern-High	Rebecca Britten
Jason Torres Rangel	R. Joseph Rodríguez
Jeanette Toomer	Ron Powers
Jimmy Santiago Baca	Taylor Deskins (and parent)
Joyce Cohen	Teri Knight
Judith A. Purvis	Tim Rollins and the following K.O.S. Members:
Katie Greene	Rick Savinon, Carlos Rivera, Victor Llanos,
Ken Burns	and Chris Hernandez
Kent D. Williamson	W. Edward Blain
Kimberly N. Parker	Winona Siegmund
Lehmann Maupin Gallery—New York	

We must also thank Tobey Antao, Vicki Boyd, Kimberly Cahill, Lisa Fowler, Anita Gildea, Alan Huisman, Sarah Fournier, Suzanne Heiser, Victoria Merecki, Cindy Black, and Bernadette Skok—all from Heinemann—for their tireless support and collaboration.

*i*ntroduction

Literature as a Bridge to Literacy

> For many students, learning to explore literature serves as a launch into practicing the literacy skills they will use for a lifetime. Powerful stories insinuate themselves in students' imaginations, making it impossible not to read on, to ask questions, to want more. It's the drive for meaning that really lights the spark for literacy learners. Once ignited, the inquiry and passion that literature evokes can light students' way into the sciences, humanities, social sciences— any and every field of disciplinary knowledge.
> —Kent D. Williamson (1957–2015), Executive Director, NCTE; Director, National Center for Literacy Education (personal communication, July 21, 2014)

Literacy. The word has been found in print and used in education in the United States since 1880, when it was used to mean one's ability to demonstrate "the quality, condition, or state of being literate; the ability to read and write. Also: the extent of this in a given community, region, period, etc." (Oxford English Dictionary). Since that time, iterations include *cultural literacy*, *digital literacy*, and *financial literacy*. Even before the Common Core State Standards, the term was growing in depth, breadth, and scope.

In today's global culture, the term no longer focuses solely on reading and writing and teaching those skills, nor is it solely the purview of elementary school. Twenty-first-century literacy now reflects what the National Center for Literacy Education describes as *literacy learning,* a concept ranging from analyzing the vast array of digital content to participating in online exchanges of information and opinion to creating virtual classrooms. This book explores how we have taught, are teaching, and will teach literature in the context of the definition of literacy provided in the National Council of Teachers of English's Position Statement "The NCTE Definition of 21st Century Literacies":

> *Literacy has always been a collection of cultural and communicative practices shared among members of particular groups. As society and technology change, so does literacy. Because technology has increased the intensity and complexity of literate environments, the 21st century demands that a literate person possess a wide range of abilities and competencies, many literacies. These literacies are multiple, dynamic, and malleable. As in the past, they are inextricably linked with particular histories, life possibilities, and social trajectories of individuals and groups. Active, successful participants in this 21st century global society must be able to:*
>
> - Develop proficiency and fluency with the tools of technology;
> - Build intentional cross-cultural connections and relationships with others so to pose and solve problems collaboratively and strengthen independent thought;
> - Design and share information for global communities to meet a variety of purposes;
> - Manage, analyze, and synthesize multiple streams of simultaneous information;
> - Create, critique, analyze, and evaluate multimedia texts;
> - Attend to the ethical responsibilities required by these complex environments.
>   (NCTE, 2013)

Complex literature stimulates *creative thinking. It educates a reader's imagination. In a world that increasingly values speed over all else, literature demands that students slow down, stop to think, pause to ponder and reflect on important questions that have puzzled mankind for a very long time.*

—Carol Jago, associate director of the California Reading and Literature Project, UCLA and past president of the National Council of Teachers of English (January 22, 2015)

The world in which our students grow is global, technological, and demanding of critical skills that require reading abilities to decipher meaning and message. Literacy and literacy learning within many disciplines is now a fundamental necessity. This focus and redefinition requires us as English language arts teachers to reflect and consider how we can use literature as a bridge to help our twenty-first-century students connect with complex topics, texts, and decisions. While this perspective may at first seem unreasonable, daunting, unnecessary, and without precedent at the secondary level, it moves us into a more relevant position than ever before. Although English language arts has always had a presence in K–12 education—consistent, substantive, and relevant—the twenty-first-century focus on and redefinition of literacy has also redefined and solidified the import of English language arts, elementary through secondary.

Like the engineers who built the steel-arteried bridges that connect us in the physical world, we are now using our knowledge of and skills with literature to provide connections no other content area can. We use literature to move, prepare, and sustain our students far beyond our immediate classrooms—beyond the seemingly isolated text. In the world of today, young people must launch themselves into adulthood with a sense of agency, able to communicate clearly with a wide variety of audiences and learn from media and communications of all forms, while embracing complexities and challenges. Whereas some may say that there is no place for literature in these circumstances, those of us who are aware of its timeless power know better. Using literature, we teach and explore and model how to read documents in everyday life: Marc Antony's funeral oration rhetorically models for our students how to craft a message that not only persuades the audience but also moves it to act physically and emotionally. Using literature, we enable our students' exploration of how an author targets audience, occasion, and purpose, the same skills students need to write a statement of purpose or fill out an application: Little Geoffrey's Prelude to *The Canterbury Tales* explaining the real motives of the pilgrims, including his own. Using literature, we enable our students' exploration of theme, style, message, giving students the tools they need to decode a candidate's position statement or an opinion piece: Scout's finding her voice, asking her father the hard questions, sending a verbal op-ed piece to his soul. Combining all these elements, literature gives us rich material to teach reading skills: decoding, critical thinking, evaluation, analysis, and inquiry.

Our students *must* possess and hone these skills as they progress from high school into college and career. The English language arts classroom is where this essential and critical literacy bridge is fomented, protected, encouraged, pushed, tempered, and forged. Using the literature we love and we understand so well, we can and must empower our students to think and reflect and evaluate independently in a very complex and multimessaged world requiring reading and comprehension at work, play, and home. As you read the chapters in this book, you will also read—*hear*—the words of educators, students, scholars, writers, journalists, civil rights activists, documentarians, artists expressing their professional and personal perspectives while responding to a query we posed: "How would you describe literature as a literacy bridge?" We want this book to be the beginning of conversation and reflection, the beginning of new ways of thinking about how we teach literature that lives outside our classrooms. In addition, students' voices and perspectives are represented here, based on an anonymous reading survey we conducted (2014–15). More than 600 students responded. These responses "peppered" throughout the book—within the text itself, as well as in sidebars—provide additional perspectives from varied and diverse walks of life, crossing race, class, gender, and age.

In my own adolescence, later in my life as a high school teacher, and now as a teacher educator, litera-ture and the communal exploration of peoples' stories have stood as a bridge to embracing the richness and complexity of my own humanity and those around me. Reading literature affords us opportunities to see ourselves through and in others, to explore new perspectives, to connect, and to question what it means to be free. (Logan Manning, assistant professor of literacy education, University of Texas, San Antonio, personal communication, January 15, 2015)

1

Taking Control of Teaching Literature in the Era of Common Core

Though the connection between access to good literature and the development of literacy has long been recognized, it is too often undervalued in schools today. Under pressure to raise test scores, many schools focus narrowly on developing language skills while ignoring the need to provide children with access to literature that might motivate and inspire them to become independent readers and lifelong learners. Great literature can ignite children's imagination, make it possible for them to explore their identity and expand their sense of what is possible. It can also be the key to empowering children to experience the power of knowledge.

—Pedro Nogura, Columbia University (personal communication, November 13, 2014)

REGARDLESS OF ONE'S POSITION on the Common Core, it has created resonating conversation and focus on English language arts (ELA) from those who do not teach ELA at the secondary level. More importantly, it has begun conversation, reflection, and rediscovery among English teachers. We have had to reconsider how we see and understand and implement what we call *English language arts*, while recognizing how literature is at the fulcrum of this conversation.

When I, Jocelyn, first began teaching, I was in awe of the ELA teachers surrounding me. I still am. One guiding passion was their certain knowledge of why they were English teachers: they were the sentinels at the gate. They were the protectors of the exposure and experience students would have with literature. I still hear this notion from some colleagues, now followed by their fear of potential loss, attrition, of voice, of control, of being listened to as an expert. New trends, ever developing and shifting state and federal policies, new and ever increasing forms

> *I actually do sometimes.*
>
> —Student response when asked, "Do you use the reading skills and strategies you have learned in your English class when not in school?"

> *The teaching profession* is a spiderweb of inter-connectivity, yet an island of isolation at the same time. For me, literature reaches out across space to connect the dots.
>
> —Emily Hamm, ELA teacher (January 10, 2015)

of reading and writing for various audiences and purposes—all are having an unprecedented impact on ELA classes and on us as ELA teachers.

Reports, beginning with President Reagan's "A Nation at Risk" through the current Common Core State Standards (2015a), along with their ensuing polices, have fomented this increased attention—rediscovery—of ELA's import and how we teach what we love—literature. We find ourselves much like Dante (Pinsky 1996): "Midway upon the journey of our life / I found myself within a forest dark, / For the straightforward pathway had been lost." This seeming confusion is really a clarifying moment. The very thing we love, literature, is the pathway, a pathway we know so well, yet we still have much to learn and discover along with our students. Exciting. Risky. Exhilarating. And, yes, daunting, indeed.

In this time of increased scrutiny, we can reclaim our voice, reaffirm our passion, reassert our expertise, and assume the responsibility of teaching, modeling, and facilitating literacy learning. Literature is a perfect vehicle for literacy learning, one that naturally transcends our classrooms.

FINDING OUR VOICES

If you had asked me years ago what threatened teachers' voices most, I would have had an easy answer: censorship. As a Twain scholar, I have been asked on numerous occasions to speak about *Adventures of Huckleberry Finn*, especially in relation to the ongoing battle, spanning more than sixty years, over whether to remove it from school libraries or retain it.

I remember a community meeting in Enid, Oklahoma, in 2000, where I spoke and then watched as a serpentine line of teachers waited their turn at the microphone to address why they defended their students' right to read Twain's work. Parents, concerned citizens, the school board—all listened to those amazing, brave, impassioned high school teachers assert their voices that evening. Although Enid did listen, ultimately deciding to keep *Huck Finn* in schools, other towns and school districts did not. Fighting these censorship battles, ELA teachers around the country were passionate, weary at times, dedicated, elastic—voices, once heard, growing fainter, practically inaudible (Emerson 1916).

When I consider the question today, the answer is less clear-cut. In my work with teachers, I have found scores of silenced voices—not because they have nothing to express, not because they feel no need to express their thoughts, and not because they have given up and/or given in. Rather, they feel stripped of power and without support—what difference would it make even if they did speak up? More and more, I hear the same concern: we care about our students, and we love what we teach, but we have no voice; no one listens. And since the release of the Common Core State Standards in 2010, public attention on ELA and the literature and other texts we teach has increased exponentially.

HOW WE GOT HERE

The responsibilities and challenges English teachers face today are the result of a range of factors. There are so many voices we must listen to, comprehend, and process before we can listen to and work with our students (who are never the same class to class and, more importantly, never the same year to year): state and local policy makers, building administrators and directors/coordinators, chief academic officers, parents, concerned citizens, interest groups, and federal policy makers. Über-multitasking—listening to diverse and wide-ranging audiences, comprehending the varied messages, determining and creating the most effective and engaging literacy learning pathways—has contextualized our approach to teaching ELA for some time now. In the midst of this political, social, and educational cacophony, we strive to maintain for our students effective, engaging, relevant curricula and learning environments. And our instructional assertion has remained stalwart, even when confronted by various challenges: our students do benefit from their experiences with literature.

Teaching literature has also assumed center stage in conversations outside our classrooms. Just recently, an article by Terry Eagleton (2015) appeared in *The Chronicle of Higher Education*. Although the article focuses on Eagleton's ideas about why universities in England are suffering, he makes an astonishing comment about the state of instruction in secondary schools (an assessment also articulated on this side of the Atlantic):

> *The effects of this sidelining of the humanities can be felt all the way down the educational system in the secondary schools where modern languages are in precipitous decline, history really means modern history, and the teaching of the classics is largely confined to private institutions such as Eton College.*

In addition to those who feel that the canon is not being taught widely, there are also those voices that herald the potential death of the canon in its classical, pristine state—Egyptian, Greek, and Roman literature, with perhaps Shakespeare and Dickens, for example—citing inclusion of diverse/multicultural literature as the primary "assault" on our students in ELA classrooms. Sandra Stotsky (1999), among others, keenly articulates her viewpoint, using children of color and poverty as symbols:

> *In order to restore the primacy of intellectual and civic goals in the reading curriculum, the public needs to understand how [multiculturalism] constitutes an assault on the development of children's language and thinking and why black and Hispanic children are likely to be among those most damaged by this assault.* (xviii)

Stotsky's argument and others like it might be valid if our goal were to structure a society in which the voices of citizens of color and poverty were to be ignored. Indeed, if we were trying to teach all of our students that "multicultural" voices were deficient, it would be logical to view those voices—especially the most persuasive and endearing of those voices—as damaging to students, as they would provide enticing models and perspectives that deviate from the norm. Of course, those are not our goals. We are aiming to build critical thinking in all of our students and to learn from the entire human experience. We dare not forget that the diversity of the ancient world has determined that our literature—even our "classical" literature—contains multicultural components. The argument that an inclusion of multicultural texts is an assault on students rings hollow when we consider how multicultural texts help us to hear voices from the past and the present in context.

I have listened to, had conversations with, and even challenged teachers describing their versions of instruction in secondary ELA classes today:

- We teach too much literature.
- We teach too little literature.
- We no longer teach classical, or canonical, texts.
- We teach too much young adult literature.
- We teach too little young adult literature.
- We teach too many diverse voices.
- We do not teach enough diverse voices.
- We do not teach any women's literature.
- We do not teach enough women's literature.

Everyone has an opinion, whatever its accuracy. Ironically, in the midst of such ongoing logomachies, ELA teachers continue to create literacy instruction, with literature as the foundational bridge.

Policy

A few historical "milestones" helped place ELA (literature particularly) in the key role they currently occupy in K–12 education. From the time of Benjamin Franklin and the Committee of Ten Report (1892) to the progressive era (1930–40s) to "A Nation at Risk" (1980s) to No Child Left Behind (2000; U.S. Department of Education) to Common Core State Standards (2010), English language arts—literature, grammar, and composition (rhetoric)—have formed the nucleus of education curricula.

Although educational policies have affected the content and impact of ELA classes, so have court rulings. In 1998, in Arizona, a decision from the United States Court of Appeals for the Ninth Circuit on *Monteiro v. The Tempe Union High School District* had far-reaching implications, fundamentally affecting every ELA classroom in the country. Writing for the majority, Circuit Judge Stephen Reinhardt rendered an opinion that would echo throughout the United

States with regard to the literature we teach. Although the opinion, excerpted below, is a response to *Adventures of Huckleberry Finn* and Faulkner's "A Rose for Emily," it encapsulates how we envision literature's power and purpose, as well as how we as ELA teachers understand its relevance to our students:

> First, the fact that a student is required to read a book does not mean that he is being asked to agree with what is in it. It cannot be disputed that a necessary component of any education is learning to think critically about offensive ideas—without that ability one can do little to respond to them. . . .
>
> *The function of books and other literary materials, as well as of education itself, is to stimulate thought, to explore ideas, to engender intellectual exchanges. Bad ideas should be countered with good ones, not banned by the courts. One of the roles of teachers is to guide students through the difficult process of becoming educated, to help them learn how to discriminate between good concepts and bad, to benefit from the errors society has made in the past, to improve their minds and characters. Those who choose the books and literature that will influence the minds and hearts of our nation's youth and those who teach young people in our schools bear an awesome responsibility. We can only encourage them to exercise their authority wisely and well, and to be sensitive to the needs and concerns of all of their students.* (Reinhardt 1998) [Italics mine]

This opinion reifies how our passionate expertise contextualizes literature's import in the classroom—"an awesome responsibility," indeed.

Demands for College and Career Readiness

A growing number of progressive parents, concerned citizens, policy makers, and students, along with social and economic trends, have played significant roles in redefining literacy learning in secondary education. This twenty-first-century perspective views educational content as a means of reinforcing students' cumulative knowledge and application of critical reading and thinking as they make decisions, decipher texts, have conversations and encounters throughout their lives. This progressive redefinition is having a profound effect on how we teach texts, both literary and informational:

> *If literacy is constructing and articulating meaning, then literature must be meaningful to our students. In our richly diverse world, it makes sense to draw on literature that represents multiple cultural perspectives and styles of communication. This helps students affirm the power of text and its relevance to their lives. Research reminds us that student motivation and student performance in reading increase when students see themselves and their communities mirrored in the literature they read. As our students*

have multiple opportunities to express what they understand about the themes or motivations behind a character and analyze worldviews that they may or may not share with characters, they are constructing meaning. In role-playing possible alternatives to the story or comparing experiences of different characters, our students are making personal and intertextual connections that promote their cognitive development and enhance their language skills. More than that, when they join in well-structured academic conversations that support the participation of all voices, they grow in their understanding and vision of the world. Using literature as a bridge to literacy, then, means using the stories, experiences, and issues in our students' worlds as the springboards for exploration and learning. It means having students write about their inquiries, discoveries, and new knowledge deriving from or leading to their reading of the literature and sharing their reflections. It means recognizing that how we see the world and communicate our perspectives about that world is cultural. It means tapping those cultural connections as various ways of deepening our knowledge and dispositions about the world. Interacting not just with the literature but with each other about the literature builds literacy. It is in the social interaction with others about the literature read, discussing what they understand, exploring possibilities, and writing about that literature that students affirm and extend their thinking and broaden their perspectives. (MaryCarmen Cruz, ELA teacher/mentor, personal communication, February 3, 2015)

Although censorship may no longer be the foremost challenge facing English teachers today, our role in combating censorship has taught us some valuable lessons that are just as true today as they were when I spoke in Enid in 2000: as ELA teachers, we must be aware of what we are teaching and why. We must be self-assured and confident in the literature we teach; we must be able to articulate for others who are not ELA educators the importance and relevance of our literature. As ELA teachers, we assume parents, administrators, policy makers, and, yes, our students intuitively understand and appreciate literature as we do. Yet, as the character Sportin' Life sings in *Porgy and Bess*, "It ain't necessarily so."

New Kinds of Texts and Students' New Relationships with Texts

We are also experiencing a shift in our students' interaction with texts, both literature and informational—texts we assign and those students elect to read. Visual and most assuredly tactile, students now have a moveable feast of text interaction options from which to choose: Kindle, Google Books, iPad, Chromebooks, an ever changing array of laptops, and, of course, hard copies. There is also a growing and diverse tapestry of texts types: picture books, graphic novels, illustrated books, speaking/interactive books (apps), and, of course, traditional texts.

In such an amazing world, we must now approach literature and informational text from a revised position. We must:

- understand this new era of students, considering their experiences, probable pastimes and activities, preferred methods of communication and entertainment
- think about why some students elect not to read assigned texts, seeking shorter, more immediate vehicles
- consider students' questioning why they should care about what we assign
- reflect on how we view literature, its purpose in our ELA classes, our delivery of it
- reflect on and consider how our instructional aims and delivery address twenty-first-century students
- reflect on how the skills we teach using literature transcend the texts and extend into other content areas and life situations
- consider whether we need to adjust our approach and delivery of texts
- revise approach and delivery based on previous considerations.

An Emphasis on Literacy Skills

We must also address the introduction of literacy and literacy learning into the secondary ELA classroom. Presently, the Common Core's and society's intensified focus on literacy, literacy learning, and ELA places us once again at the forefront of instructional change. Our need for reflection is even more important now that the entire nature of literacy is shifting. Literacy learning is beginning to resonate in secondary ELA classes and in other content areas. One has only to read the Next Generation Science Standards and College, Career, & Civic Life C3 Framework for Social Studies State Standards to realize this shift and redefinition (see http://ngss .nsta.org/About.aspx and www.socialstudies.org/c3).

> *In the true* sense of literacy, it [television's informational and documentary programming, for example] can only sponsor and promote curiosity through quality work, but I think we must leave room for a new conception of literacy—as rigorous as before, that acknowledges a new and growing subset dependent on visual signs and symbols.
>
> —Ken Burns, documentarian
> (November 11, 2014)

Once the purview of elementary teachers, literacy and literacy learning are beginning to permeate K–12 instruction, the intent being to affect directly college, career readiness, and life skills. Our classes demand a great many reading and critical skills, actions and engagement that we as ELA teachers love and wholly believe are relevant on their own. Challenging us now, however, is the need to explain not only why literature provides relevant and immediate learning experiences but also how abundant shortcuts to reading abound, Sirens and Calypso luring students to certain disaster.

Students Who Aren't Reading

In the halcyon days of teaching English that we believe must have existed or that we imagined when we envisioned what teaching English would be like, we assigned the classic, canonical texts, students read them, discussed them, composed amazing essays, and all was right with the world. Sherri Bell (2004) describes this idyllic vision:

> The classroom is quiet except for the sounds of a page being flipped and the murmur of students discussing a novel's theme. The teacher circulates, facilitating discussion or asking a thoughtful question, as the students actively and willingly engage in reading. In teacher utopia, students love to read and do so well. (36)

Did that time ever exist? At any rate, as Bell surmises, "I do not live in that world" (36). Have there always been students who are voracious readers and eager students—like English majors—and students who may or may not have liked to read all the time? Or students who like, even love, to read but who have an aversion to assigned texts? I suspect the truth is in the middle. What we do know is that our twenty-first-century student audiences, as a whole, may read but do not necessarily read the entirety of what we assign.

Many articles and books have explored this dilemma; educators such as Irene Fountas and Gay Su Pinnell, Robert Probst, Robert Scholes, Carol Jago, Judith Langer, Louise Rosenblatt, Linda Darling-Hammond, and Kelly Gallagher have explored reasons our students don't find reading as exciting and as engaging as we want them to. Others such as Wayne Booth, Kenneth Burke, Richard Lanham, and Edward P. J. Corbettt have explored deeper, sustained ways for students to engage with texts. But increasingly, our students do not connect what and how they read in ELA classrooms with relevance to their own lives once they walk out the door.

ELA teachers, the most effective and immediate observers and respondents of student reading, have also noted the decline in our students' excitement and engagement with regard to the literature we assign. Among the most disturbing effects of this lack of engagement is that students' reading experiences in school do indeed indelibly shape and sometimes contort their adult reading behavior.

Alisa Belzer's (2002) insightful article "'I Don't Crave to Read': School Reading and Adulthood" throws this concern into sharp relief by

> *Teachers can effectively* use literature to help students navigate the digital landscape to construct knowledge and develop skills. At times, it seems a perilous journey; however, it can yield boundless rewards. As a literacy bridge, literature should inspire conversation that lives beyond the classroom, that removes the pressures of sitting up straight and watching the clock.
>
> —Teri Knight, ELA teacher (January 16, 2015)

exploring how five African American women describe their reading lives. All the women recount being disconnected from reading in school—"get stuck a lot," "gonna make another mistake on another word," "hard to maintain concentration," "didn't like to read, but don't know why," "I would glance through it [book]" (108, 110). All but one remember reading at home as children, though not consistently. Although all the women, as adults, do read in some fashion, one astutely summed up the feeling of all: "I don't crave to read" (108). Participants Mattie, Polly, Tamika, Laura, and Diane expressed these and similar memories and feelings when queried about their individual reading experiences in school. Belzer's conclusion is prescient, as she echoes Freire:

> These women's earlier education experience did not teach them to read the world (Freire 1983), nor did it give them access to the pleasures of reading. . . . Learners need opportunities to explore the relationship between using and creating texts that are interesting, engaging, informing, practical, and self-chosen and that have the potential to improve their literacy skills. In other words learners need to see how reading and writing in the outside-school frame can be used effectively to improve their literacy skills inside school. (112)

For teachers and all of us who care about improving the quality of K–12 education, there are critical fundamental questions: Why aren't our students voracious readers? What can we do to inspire and excite them to read in our classes and outside? How can we present the reading skills we teach so that our students will use them in their academic and everyday lives? Addressing those crucial questions and providing insights relative to their solution is the mission of this chapter and those to follow.

WHAT'S NEXT?

The policies affecting ELA necessarily foment a changing, protean approach to teaching literature. As ELA teachers, we must reassert our voices, based on our expertise, our passion, and our certain knowledge that what we teach is essential to our students inside and outside their classrooms. We must help others understand that the literature and the concomitant skills employed within ELA provide life lessons and abilities throughout college and career. We must take control of our content and instruction

Students' responses to the question, "Why may you not read the entire text?"

I don't get involved in the book so I don't read it because I can't get into it.
—tenth-grade student, Midwest

It doesn't interest you or capture your attention. You get lost in the reading. You don't understand the text.
—eleventh-grade student, West Coast

I mean, if the book is good I will continue reading it, but I will skip sections of it for the same reason.
—tenth-grade student, West Coast

once more, not hesitate to account for our approaches, not be reticent about explaining them to anyone, especially, our students. But what does this taking control look, sound, and read like in today's ELA classrooms? The place to begin is with our own perspectives.

Considering what our students need from us and what the public demands of us, casting ourselves as the sentinels at the gate places us at odds with both our students and our society. Considering ourselves literacy learners as well as literacy teachers, however, affords us the opportunity to give our students the skills they need while also leveraging the power of literature and our own considerable content knowledge. The essential difference between our being the sentinel at the gate and literacy learner/teacher lies with stasis/passivity versus protean/proactive. The difference is a little like that between transitive and intransitive verbs: Freire (2000) describes static teaching as banking—"an act of depositing, in which the students are the depositories and the teacher is the depositor" (106):

> In the banking concept of education, knowledge is a gift bestowed by those who consider themselves knowledgeable upon those whom they consider to know nothing. [Such projection] negates education and knowledge as process of inquiry. (107)

In lieu of being protectors and dispensers of literature, English teachers can enable and empower students to wrestle with a text, break it apart, explore it, experience it, and live it. From this perspective, we can use literature to transform our students into sentinels who own and practice critical reading, writing, collaborating, speaking, and listening to become critical thinkers in and outside the classroom, in their community and beyond it.

The primary reason I love working in high school classrooms is to experience this protean, messy, wonderful process. We can become so focused on our content that we don't always allow ourselves the joy and excitement of learning with our students—freeing them and ourselves to drill further, inquire more deeply, forgo answers. Our students assume we are the experts, that we know all there is to know. We must tell them we do not have all the answers, that we, too, are still learning, still asking questions. And then we settle in to explore and wrestle with the literature and learn so much from them.

How do we best take our students, our companions, throughout time and space to where the stars end so we may find what the mind knew and the heart hoped all along was there?

—Angela Baldwin, ELA teacher
(February 12, 2015)

I remember vividly a day I spent at W. T. White High School, in Dallas, when an English teacher invited me to talk to her class about Hawthorne's *The Scarlet Letter*. She was concerned that as one of the few white ELA teachers in a predominately African American school, she was not conveying literature in a way that made her students want to read it.

The school was a cacophony of loud voices, bells, and sounds, and I wondered how students could learn in such an environment. I flashed back to a *Star Trek* episode, "The Mark of Gideon," in which the *Enterprise* travels to the planet Gideon, reputed to be a paradise. Captain Kirk and his crew soon realize that paradise, too, has consequences: no bacteria, no disease, equal vast overpopulation—wall-to-wall people—no silence, no time to think, just restricted but constant movement. A traditional sentinel at the gate might long for this kind of orderliness, but if we are to be in the business of helping students to become thoughtful, critical learners who are self-determined enough to succeed in today's world, orderliness and compliance are not our highest goals. We must aim for engagement, for independence, and for relevance.

I entered the classroom where the students were waiting. Together, we settled in to share, explore, and discuss this novel, and the outside world melted away; we were in our own space and time, working our way through Hester Prynne, Chillingworth, Dimmesdale, the infamous scarlet *A*, and mercurial Pearl.

The conversation was give-and-take, Socratic, privileging their voices and questions and assessments. One young man asked, "Why does Dimmmmmmesdale have to be so dumb?" We saw his point immediately and laughed. Together we experienced this decidedly nineteenth-century novel—condensed-extended metaphor and all—as never before. The most wonderful and memorable moment was discussing the "dreaded" description of the *A*. I have had students complain, sigh, disregard, and openly criticize Hawthorne's style—too long, no reason, stupid, dumb, really?—I've heard it all. On this day, the students, both young men and ladies, associated the description with quilting. Talking about the quilts some of their grandmothers had made and given their families, they connected the intricacies of Hester's *A* with artifacts many of them saw every day. One student, a young lady, said, "Say, this is like that character in that book—*Beloved*, right? And the author's black, right?" Instead of recoiling at Hawthorne's long description, these students wove this literary work into their own lives.

> *Apart from a* rare few, the young people I teach *do not pick up literature with much enthusiasm. . . . They always hope that if they complain enough, I will abandon the text for something simpler. Instead I assure them that over the next few weeks I will show them how to unlock this text for themselves. I let students know that the satisfaction they will feel at meeting this textual challenge is an intellectual reward that I would not for the world deny them.*
>
> —Carol Jago (2011, xvii)

The Scarlet Letter is difficult under most circumstances, even for college students. And not all the students had read up to the point assigned. But some had done so and had questions. These questions made the others curious, and our discussions fueled further curiosity. Students began comparing actions of the characters with their own realities, thereby making meaning relevant for them.

> *A novel can (ought) to make available more in-sight into a subject by delving into human character as it responds to social and historical forces. . . . Fiction can parallel history, but it is not history.*
>
> —Toni Morrison, author (in response to students in my Twain, Faulkner, Morrison class, 2001[1])

For me this experience symbolizes the power of literature, the potential of our students when allowed to stretch and explore, and the role of the ELA teacher in binding and kneading all the elements together. That day Nathaniel Hawthorne's *The Scarlet Letter* created a bridge to literacy learning—it opened up a pathway for students to exercise their voices and opinions. They took a risk with me, and we dived into a very difficult book.

Do I know for a fact they all completed the novel? No. I do know, however, that each of us was affected by our sharing and by the author and his characters. Many of these students, some who may have shared the same reticence for or flat-out rejection of reading as the five women in Belzer's "I Don't Crave to Read" (2002), for a moment read and discussed and related this novel to their own lives and experiences. Because one student remembered reading *Beloved* and made a connection, others may have decided to read that book for themselves. Even if some didn't complete Hawthorne's book, all had glimpsed literature as something that could be meaningful in their own lives. As Anne Ruggles Gere describes this bridging process:

> C. S. Lewis wrote that literature doesn't simply describe reality; it adds to it. Much of what it adds is imagination and new ways of seeing the world. These qualities make literature a bridge to the vast variety of cultural and communicative practices that we call literacy. (personal communication, November 9, 2014)

English teachers have always known and subscribed to the power of literature. In so many ways, ELA teachers are born and then later educated and trained. No one compels us to read. No one creates a map or a Venn diagram for us to see the place in the text. No one draws or illustrates for us the characters so that we can see them. No one provides audio support so we can hear the tone and intent. For us, literature is a beloved natural. This passion is our strength; it can also be our Achilles' heel, if we do not understand how to channel our passion to serve our twenty-first-century students. We think nothing of comparing a challenging situation, event, or decision to a piece of literature. We think in metaphor. Many of our students do not, or at least, they don't think they do. But once they learn these and other skills through experiences with literature, they can use them to navigate other courses, college, their career, and their everyday

---

1. I frequently asked writers, teachers, and curriculum coordinators to speak to my students—all of whom intended to teach high school. Although Professor Morrison had helped in a previous year, she again agreed to help my students as they were teaching her works in their student teaching.

lives—remember the quilt? Sixty percent of students responded yes to the reading survey statement "Literature provides me with information about other cultures, times, and challenges, but also it allows me to expand my literary skills beyond the classroom," and some explicated their responses for clarity:

> *This statement is true, because outside of school I wouldn't want to read [anything] besides gossip magazines, but reading in class has opened my mind to seeing other people's perspectives in the world besides mine.*
> —eleventh-grade student, West Coast

> *I would agree completely with the first part and partly agree with the second part, because I don't know how analyzing Shakespeare and other literature like it will expand my literacy skills beyond the classroom.*
> —twelfth-grade student, Southwest

> *I think this is true because the more you learn about literature then you realize that some of the way you use the English language is dumb.*
> —eleventh-grade student, Southwest

This isn't to say that learning alongside students and letting their questions and ideas guide your work is simple, easy, or quick. Even in my work with other ELA teachers—dedicated, brilliant, well-educated professionals—I see how challenging this approach can be, but also how rewarding it so often is.

I recently conducted a teacher workshop in Hannibal, Missouri, "Teaching Tom Sawyer and Huckleberry Finn, and Common Core Standards with Mark Twain." My goal for the sessions was to model taking students through these difficult period texts. As John Spencer (2012) says in "Don't Bribe My Kids to Read," the journey was not always easy or pleasant. I asked many probative questions; I waited for responses. No quizzes, no short-answer essays, no fill-in-the-blanks. We collaborated, shared, inquired, and, yes, challenged. We were all the better for it. No one was the same teacher at the conclusion of the workshop as at the beginning, including me.

I draw strength from the shift in perspective that comes with seeing myself as a learner rather than a traditional sentinel. Despite being a Mark Twain scholar, I am not—I should say, was not—fond of *The Adventures of Tom Sawyer*. I revised this egregious error when the Shrewsbury (Massachusetts) Public Library asked me to present this novel for their "Big Read" in 2012. As I grudgingly reread the novel, the text unfolded in a new way. Instead of indulging my predispositions and points of view, I allowed the text to speak to me, practiced what I so earnestly preach: read the text for what it says, not for what you think it says, what you want it to say, how you want to contrive it. When we help our students make meaningful connections and address their own curiosities and confusions, we relinquish our ownership of the text; we let it speak to them directly. One of the Hannibal workshop teachers, Ramah Troutman, expresses it this way:

It is necessary to connect students to the reading before we begin to read if we want them to be suc-
cessful. Making this vital connection means students can approach reading in the right frame of mind.
By framing Tom Sawyer to the student experience, by making text-to-text, text-to-self, and text-to-world
connections, students can perceive what they read. By framing the text and taking prior knowledge into
consideration, my students can approach Tom Sawyer in a meaningful way. I consider these three types
of prior knowledge especially important: (1) knowledge about the topic, (2) knowledge about the struc-
ture and organization of the text, and (3) knowledge about the vocabulary. (personal communication,
February 3, 2015)

What I have loved about ELA teachers all my life has been our resilience melded with our
embrace of change and difference, our passion, and our steely determination to keep a firm grasp
on literature to share it with all our students—through equity, access, exposure, and expanse of
perspective. These traits are in our collective DNA, regardless of region, ethnicity, class, education, gender, and whatever other codification we might name.

HOW THIS BOOK CAN HELP

The chapters that follow discuss ways in which we can take control of how we teach literature,
even when we feel bombarded by mandates and judgments. They address some of the current
forces shaping literacy education in the English classroom: the outside commentary—in the
media, in politics, in society—that is pushing into our work; the focus on informational texts;
and the fight to help our students see the meaning and relevance of the literature we love.
Along the way, we include tools useful in our work and in the work we've done with teachers
across the country:

1. **The Student Survey** (Chapter 2, page 30; Appendix A). Results of this anonymous survey
   inform how we approach the assigned literature and alert us to potential impediments—
   reading reticence, vocabulary issues, sensitive topics—we can proactively address. It's a
   reflective and honest way to learn about our students and their reading habits. Through
   both objective and subjective questions, we find out what our students feel, think, and
   perceive about their learning.
2. **Student Journals** (Chapter 2, page 32). Keeping journals gives students an opportunity to
   make their own connections, whether studying vocabulary or the big-picture themes in a
   literary work or unit. Journals integrate beautifully with collaborative learning communities, allowing students to think independently as well as collaboratively.
3. **Collaborative Learning Communities** (Chapter 2, page 33). Regardless of generational
   characteristics—Millennials through Generation Z—middle school and high school

students have similar concepts of friendships, acquaintances, and student–teacher relationships. Collaborative learning communities that are sustained throughout the year encourage and foment collaborative thinking and analysis and are an excellent vehicle for facilitating guided, independent, and collaborative reading.

4. **Close Reading and Analysis Guide** (Chapter 3, page 58; Appendix B). This guide prompts students to consider specific literary and rhetorical elements in texts and spurs them on to deeper thinking.

5. **Close Reading Analysis Evaluation Rubric** (Chapter 3, page 58; Appendix C). This tool, informed by research and refined in my work with other teachers, helps us monitor students' comprehension and critical thinking without excessive interruption in their work or our schedules.

6. **Rereading Template** (Chapter 4, page 66; Appendix D). Our love of literature is both our strength and our Achilles' heel: we sometimes fail to recognize how others are not similarly enthralled. Before teaching any unit or work—even those we know well—we can use this template to consider how the material will appear to our students. This exercise in perspective is immensely helpful as we consider our goals and our approach.

7. **Students' Literary Analysis Rubric** (Chapter 4, page 73; Appendix E). A primary goal of ELA teachers is for the literature we teach to impact our students' construction of meaning throughout their lives. We want to share our love and enjoyment and help our students see literature as a viable, reliable, and relevant vehicle that will serve them well past their time with us in a variety of settings, encounters, challenges, and expectations. Used during independent reading or a unit of study, this rubric encourages students to explore, discover, and research their own interpretations and comprehension. It also enables us to discover in real time what students don't understand that we may need to reinforce or review.

8. **Form for Selecting Texts to Pair or Blend** (Chapter 5, page 87; Appendix F). Many of us lament the pressure we feel to teach informational texts, arguments, even young adult literature. This template helps us consider how we can use these texts to support and deepen rather than supplant literature in our classrooms.

9. **What Do You Think?** (Chapter 5, page 94). This set of student-focused questions allows students to privilege their own voice and ideas while relying on our knowledge, guidance, and facilitation. This student–teacher/teacher–student learning relationship engenders a cumulative, lifelong path toward literacy. Students compare, contrast, evaluate, analyze, distinguish, enumerate, classify, and synthesize the literary text and their relationship with it.

10. **Essential Teacher Resources** (Appendix G). This is a compilation of some of our favorite resources on a range of topics, from poetry collections to teaching strategies and lesson plans. Putting these tools to use as early as possible in the school year helps establish the tone of the classroom as rigorous, respectful of students, and collaborative. Our collective hope is that we will create an extended professional learning community that continues the conversation.

As an educator, when I reflect on how literature is a bridge to literacy, I realize I must first clarify for myself my perception of literacy. Literacy is not just reading and writing; it encompasses and develops one's knowledge, skills, and dispositions about the world. It is a way of making and communicating meaning. Using literature as a bridge to literacy means helping the learner make connections between her world and other worlds. That happens when we are open to diverse perspectives. My grandmother would say, "Cada cabeza es un mundo"—literally translated, "Each head is a world." She declared that to her children to help them understand why the actions or thinking of acquaintances, friends, or even some family members seemed mysterious to the observer. She was passing her wisdom on to her children and grandchildren, creating understanding about human nature. Doesn't literature also provide us with that wisdom? It is human nature to want to learn, to grow, to improve one's conditions, to enjoy the beauty of life, to ask questions like "Where is my place in the world? How do I make sense of the chaos around me and how can I make a difference?" Exploring these questions through literature provides the opportunity for all learners to make meaning of the world. (MaryCarmen Cruz, ELA teacher/mentor, personal communication, February 3, 2015)

■

Literacy learning is the by-product of finding a great read. It happens almost effortlessly....And reaching for the ineffable, as Toni Morrison once said, becomes a reality. How this happens—this connection between the writer's imagination and the soul of the reader—is the hallmark of great works of literature. (Jeanette Toomer, ELA teacher, personal communication, January 20, 2015)

2 Framing Our Expectations for Literature and Our Students

After the school told my parents that my brother and I were not learning to read and were probably mildly retarded and might have to go to a special school, my parents started reading to us every night at bedtime. They read us *Tarzan of the Apes* and Bomba the Jungle Boy, among others. I remember *Merrylegs*, about a rocking horse worn out with playing, dumped, and then retrieved and restored by a kindly man for another child. I remember Skipper, a Navy dog that lost his back legs and the ship's mechanics made him a trolley so he could walk. . . .

For most of my life, my father repeated to me one of his favorite sayings: "Reading is a bloodless substitute for Living." In college, I had to undergo something very close to a nervous breakdown to become an English major in the middle of my junior year. The bridge for me was not what he said; that was a wall. It was what my parents *did* by making time stop in books that had messages that inspired me. Because of that, reading, to me, *is* living. It is a safe and secure place where I feel comfort in the experience.

I went on to teach my students to respect their responses to what they read. To notice how they respond. To then try to discover *why* they respond that way. Depending on their school level, they need to explain what they feel emotionally in terms of the events; then to state what they feel ethically, trying to capture the essence of events; next, to try to analyze how the author got them to believe something by creative skills in writing and the devices of the writers' trade, and, finally, at the top level, to understand how critics respond, and to accept or reject those responses based on all the information they can assemble. As often as not, I don't agree with the critics, and my students need to know that. That was the bear that wasn't: he wasn't "a silly man with a fur coat who needed a shave," like the bosses said he was; he was a bear! The process is, for me, a continuum; it is a whole; and it derives from my parents sitting at my bedside reading to me.

ps: I turned out not to be retarded. By seventh grade I was reading at the eleventh-grade level.

—David E. E. Sloane, University of New Haven (personal communication, January 19, 2015)

REMEMBER PARENTS' DAY? Of course you do. Schools still have Parents' Day. One memory from a particular Parents' Day in elementary school has stayed with me. My father, who was president of the PTA, held a doctorate in mathematics, and had taught at a historically black university before I was born, sat quietly in my fifth-grade mathematics class. My teacher, Mr. Penny, announced, "Today, class, we are going to review fractions. Each of you will come to the board to solve the problems there." I hated fractions. I sat there petrified, knowing Mr. Penney would call on me. He did. "Jocelyn, come to the board, please, and solve problem 3." I passed my father, smiling at him as I did, thinking, "Lord, just let me solve it, please!" I was so nervous I miscalculated, did not recheck my work, and turned around, signaling to Mr. Penny that I had finished. Before Mr. Penny could say anything, my father said quietly, "Jocelyn Ann, look again at the problem." My classmates froze; I felt trapped; my father was patient and waiting. "Yes, sir." I turned to the board, taking a deep breath. As I now solved the problem correctly, everyone except my father gave a sigh of relief. At dinner, my father and mother and I revisited the day, and my father explained to me about expectations—his and my mother's for me, now and in the future.

From that moment on, I understood the term *expectations* and what it meant for me in the context of my parents. My parents—and grandparents—so believed in and modeled their perspective of expectations that the words *respect, high achievement, ever striving, honor, duty,* and, most importantly, *humility* became and are yet my watchwords. Every day, every experience, every conversation, my parents and I lived and loved within this context. This life experience has translated into my teaching and into my expectations of my students. We can and should, even must, set our expectations high for all students.

Too often in recent years, I have heard and read disturbing comments about "types" of students who cannot

My father always told me I was wasting my time in art. How can I be wasting my time when I got a painting hanging in the Museum of Modern Art?

Figure 2.1
Detail from Kids of Survival's interpretation of Kafka's *The Metamorphosis*

—Kids of Survival (K.O.S.) student/artist Carlos Rivera (*Kids of Survival*, 1996 documentary)

aspire to excel because of the usual factors: ethnicity, class, socioeconomic status. As ELA teachers we know a certain and irrefutable truth better than most: if we wait until discrimination in all its iterations disappears, if we wait until we live in a class-blind society, if we wait until everyone enjoys an equitable and comfortable socioeconomic status, we might as well close our books, turn off the lights, and lock our classroom doors. We dare not hold our students who depend on us, K–12, hostage to real concerns over which we have no control. Our high expectations for our students and ourselves have the power to move our students. Imagine if we all subscribed to this philosophy regardless of external factors?

The expectations we convey to students extend far beyond our classrooms. John recalls a chilling comment he heard from a young man he interviewed in South Central Los Angeles. There was true danger in the air. The young man's words were laced with profanity, not because he was trying to impress John but because he was expressing his anger, his lack of expectations, and his searing vision of an empty future. "You wanna know what's going on—nothing. I ain't worth shit, none of us are worth shit, and we ain't never gonna be more than shit." Totally lacking expectations. Provocative. Tragic. To this day, John talks about the far-reaching implications of that interview not only for him but also for the teen.

Twain's thoughts on the impact of "good literature" taught by "good teachers":

> [Students] are taught that the true motives of life are to reach for the highest ideals. . . . And best of all, they are taught to act for themselves and to think for themselves. It is this self-thinking that goes to make up the true public opinion. (1907, 658)

What happens when a teacher has and maintains expectations of students, even if they may not have them at home or in their community? In 1981, artist and teacher Tim Rollins decided he wanted to meld his talent for art and his passion for teaching. His first group was middle school students in New York's South Bronx, who would eventually identify themselves as Kids of Survival (K.O.S.). These students had been labeled unteachable, special needs, disinterested, difficult, impossible to teach. With Rollins' guidance, these students used texts to inspire their artwork, and the resulting pieces are in public collections in museums such as the Lehmann Maupin Gallery, New York's Museum of Modern Art, London's Tate Gallery, Maine's Portland Museum of Art, and Boston's Museum of Fine Arts. I initially "met" K.O.S. in the Portland Museum of Art. I was so taken with their interpretation of Mark Twain's Jim that I immediately researched the first iteration of the group: Tim Rollins, Carlos Rivera, Victor Llanos, Chris Hernandez, and Rick Savinon.

K.O.S.' rules codify the expectations Rollins establishes and maintains. He models these expectations and exacts them consistently and coherently. Many books and exhibit catalogues detailing the history and art of K.O.S. have been published, but in the documentary *Kids of Survival: The*

> **There are all** *these temptations that can lead you from the group; it's so easy, I can make $2,000 a week just by pressing a little button, advising someone upstairs a cop is coming. And I choose not to because I'm an artist, and that's what I want to be.*
>
> —K.O.S. student/artist Carlos Rivera (*Kids of Survival*, 1996 documentary)

Art and Life of Tim Rollins + K.O.S. (1996), one hears and sees and experiences the teens and the student–teacher/teacher–student learning relationship. Rollins explains that no criminal activity is permitted inside or outside the workshop, and the kids themselves list the other expectations:

- Can't be on drugs.
- Have to be in school and have a C average.
- Can't have babies.

A stalwart structure emerges in an arrangement that might initially appear to an outsider to lack any structure at all. Expectations, rules, responsibility, accountability—for many of these young people, their very first exposure to these concepts—combine to create an instructional pathway toward each teen's completion of secondary school and then entry into college and career. With rigorous expectations conducive for creating a bridge to literacy, anchored in literature and art, these students experience ownership and a vested interest in their own learning. To complete his literacy bridge, Rollins relies on canonical and contemporary literature and informational/nonfiction texts as a required instructional context for students creating their art.

Expectedly, students' most difficult literacy learning challenge is the reading requirement. To create art based on these texts, each K.O.S. member must read the literature or informational piece, which provides the thematic context, before any artwork begins. Rollins and students collaboratively read and discuss each text, referring back to the text often as they work. Just as ELA teachers are concerned about and are attuned to our students' learning and access differences, especially with regard to literature, Rollins has combined elements of the traditional secondary ELA curriculum, pairing literature and informational texts with his students' love of and talent for creating art. High expectations indeed.

ELA teachers have always known students can and will rise to our expectations. However, the present clamoring of so many outside voices sometimes drowns us out. But make no mistake, high expectations are necessary for all students—underachieving, middle-of-the road, and high-performing. And while we may not be one hundred percent successful one hundred percent of the time, we still must push our students for the twelve sequential years we have them. Our instructional expectations for our students and the literature we select for them are determined by answering three essential questions:

1. Is the literature really too hard, too remote, too disconnected for twenty-first-century students who are not in honors, advanced placement, or gifted and talented courses and who do not have parents who encourage and model reading in the home?

2. What are our expectations for all our students? Are those expectations equal?

3. What strategies and approaches can we explore to realize our expectations for all our students?

As teachers, our expectations for students are two-pronged: first, in class for the academic year we share with them and second, after they move on and leave the school for the world.

WHAT DO WE MEAN BY HIGH EXPECTATIONS?

When I enter classrooms today—secondary and college—I expect to immerse students in the literature and the period and circumstances that birthed it. However, my expectations don't end there. I expect the students to:

- be familiar with the assigned text
- have read particular sections at my prior request
- be curious
- bring their honest, uncensored views, concerns, and questions about the text
- engage in collaborative, honest, reflective conversation—no restrictions
- without exception participate as a class and individually
- have total respect for different perspectives and be willing to wrestle with these ideas.

When they put that A on Hester Prynne, like instead of hiding it, she showed it to everybody, and I feel that was her A, that's what she felt, that was her feeling. So, for me that's like, that's me, that's my A, that's what I think of myself.

Figure 2.2
Kids of Survival's *Hester at Her Needle*

—K.O.S. student/artist Victor Llanos (*Kids of Survival*, 1996 documentary)

My aim is not to create ELA majors; it is to create micro- and macroconundrums for students. I want students to lose themselves in a text and then wrestle with it to ascertain why and how this text speaks to their reality. Our students do not need to remember lines from Shakespeare, but rather reflect on and consider the moments when, in their own wrestling with texts, they hit upon ideas, impressions, and solutions that may, at some point, relate to them. Then, long after they have left our classrooms, they can apply the kind of analytical thinking they practiced in these moments to the conundrums of their daily life.

As English teachers, we do not expect students to agree with us but to have their own ideas, try them out, support them, convince others of them, or adjust or completely change them in the face of new ideas and evidence. Even though I feel ready to spiral up to the ceiling in agitation when some students tell me that they "really like" Dimmesdale, my goal is not to convince students of my opinion; it is always to foment critical thinking.

From this perspective, ethnicity, culture, class, gender, religion, politics, geographical region, or age do not have the power to separate reader and text. Drilling into a literary text from a variety of learning pathways individually and collaboratively necessarily opens new possibilities for students, and more often than not they realize that their experiences and challenges, relationships, aspirations and fears, accomplishments and struggles, although unique to them, are still part of the same human tapestry of living woven into literature.

CAN ALL STUDENTS MEET HIGH EXPECTATIONS WHEN READING LITERATURE?

Expectations are key objectives for ELA teachers; they are not, however, always equal for all students. Sometimes we, too, succumb to the notion of what students cannot do. Sometimes these notions are based on ethnicity and/or class. Sometimes we read behavioral issues as a lack of ability. Interestingly, we succumb *because* we care, because we do not want to hurt our students, and because we do not want our students to feel singled out or pushed to an extent that may be viewed as being too hard or too high by someone unfamiliar with the relationship. Nevertheless, when we take on the responsibility for determining who is and is not able to succeed, we may make serious missteps.

In my early years of teaching, I participated in a conversation that included an elementary teacher who was also the parent of two children who had been my students in previous years. We respected each other, and she had trusted me with her children. As a group of colleagues sat talking one afternoon, this teacher mentioned that it was her common practice to retain students of color in second grade because "they" were never prepared to move on to the challenges of third grade. I was stunned and astounded.

I mention this not because I believe the practice to have been typical, then or now. But I have observed something similar emerge at the secondary level. For many reasons—media coverage, stereotypes, economics—even objective and caring teachers can codify our students and selectively limit the literature we teach. A colleague once earnestly explained that classical texts, including Shakespeare, were simply "too high a hurdle" for some students because of poverty, ethnicity, and experience. He continued that having such expectations for these students would be unfair to them, that we were dooming them to inescapable failure. I disagreed then, and I certainly disagree now.

Some of my graduate students have expressed similar concerns and positions. One said that no children of color or living in poverty would ever meet rigorous expectations until poverty in the United States has been completely addressed and eliminated. I asked him (and the rest of the class), "So what are we to do in the interim? Forgo the education we know we should provide?" One young woman replied, "Yes, because we cannot make these students feel they can never compete or embarrass them in class." Another cautioned "We should be careful here. Are we qualified to determine what students can and cannot learn?" Someone else maintained, "Well, we will be qualified, so yes, we will be able to determine that; of course, we will." I repeated my question differently: "So do we allow students to linger behind and not receive the same caliber and rigor of education?" With many furrowed brows, we concluded that although we wished poverty could be totally eliminated in the United States, we could not wait for that to happen to provide equitable education for all students. From this assertion, we then proceeded to explore what we could do.

Figure 2.3

Kids of Survival's interpretation of Orwell's *Animal Farm*. This fresh interpretation of a highly political work is a model for the kind of critical and creative thinking we want our students to master, not only when they read Orwell's work but also when they read other texts, such as Shakespeare's political plays, and experience other social and political events.

OVERCOMING OBSTACLES TO MEETING HIGH EXPECTATIONS

We surveyed over six hundred high school students from across the country to find out how today's students connect with literature. The results revealed that even reticent readers and students who said some of the texts were too difficult did not say they did not want to read or that they hated reading. Two-thirds of them did mention a seeming lack of connection, a fear of being wrong, a fear of being laughed at, and a fear of not knowing as much as their peers.

Observing the reading habits of my remedial, regular, and honors students, I saw that some of them were not embracing the assigned texts, regardless of ethnicity, class, gender, experience, family dynamics, and ability. They were not identifying with the texts because I had failed to lay the groundwork.

The first year I taught Shakespeare's *The Tragedy of Julius Caesar* to my class of remedial students, I believed that if I read it aloud or used a recording, they would at least understand the plot, characters, and conflict. The language was an obvious barrier, but I thought their hearing the words would overcome that obstacle. It did not. Only after a year of trial and error spent learning from my students was I able to redesign my approach. With the experience I'd gained and the perseverance and trust of my next group of remedial students, I again attempted

Shakespeare's play. During the summer I reread the text, reviewed the comments of my previous students, and identified the factors I needed to address:

- Introduce the *idea of drama*—its purpose, its setting, what watching a play on the stage would look like, feel like. (I used playbills and posters and compared and contrasted it with their favorite TV shows.)
- Identify and discuss familiar elements that would encourage and guide their reading: jealousy, power, gifts (wills and testaments, funerals), aggression/fighting, anger, friendship, payback (retribution).
- Overcome the perceived barrier of the play's length by approaching it in chunks.
- Use a combination of my reading aloud, listening to a recording, and immediately discussing what they just heard.
- List the primary characters on the board every day, along with a brief précis of each character's role/position.
- Distribute a brief list of recurring words with which students would likely be unfamiliar, with a contemporary paraphrase next to it. (We added to this list as we worked our way through the play. Students loved being able to voice their bewilderment, disagreement, curiosity, and sheer disdain without my judging or criticizing them.)
- Focus on just two themes this time: jealousy and aggression (retribution).
- Use images so students could "see" the characters.
- Focus on a single figure of speech this time, simile.
- Constantly identify and discuss the themes' relevance.
- Have the students keep individual journals that they shared and discussed daily. (This allowed me to gauge their interest and understanding in real time.)

Before I even mentioned Shakespeare, I worked through more engaging, young-adult-friendly, contemporary works and a set of folktales, creating a trajectory of reading at a pace my students could manage. This wasn't just a matter of reading "easy" texts before "hard" ones; it was basic training. They had opportunities to analyze, argue, and defend viewpoints

> **When students learn** that none of Shakespeare's original manuscripts exist and that we're not sure exactly what he wrote, they feel liberated. The fact that the text is not set in stone somehow allows them to feel less intimidated about reading Shakespeare.
> —Michael LoMonico, Senior Consultant on National Education at the Folger Shakespeare Library (April 20, 2015)

regarding more accessible texts more clearly similar to their lives. By the time we began Shakespeare, my students were able to ratchet up the skills they had strengthened earlier in the year. By the time we finished *Julius Caesar*, they felt a sense of accomplishment.

I used this same preparation for my nonremedial students, adjusting my responses to each class. Even though the paths were different for each class—and, in some cases, for each student—every student was able to meet the expectation that they read *Julius Caesar* and wrestle with the ideas in it.

While it would take an entire book (or more!) to identify every possible academic obstacle, every impediment to meeting high expectations, there are a few things we can do to make literature more accessible to our students. They are discussed next.

Make the Vocabulary Familiar

If students are not familiar with the words in a text or don't understand familiar words being used in a different context, they won't be able to meet our high expectations for critical thought. We must reread a text each time we assign it, looking for words we know will trip them up—from *zounds* in *Henry IV* to *boarding-house* in *Huck Finn*. Especially troublesome are words that look familiar but have unfamiliar meanings in context (*humor* has a very different meaning in Elizabethan literature, for example).

The best tool for helping students embrace new words is not a list or glossary of words handed out at the start of a unit but a vocabulary journal, physical or digital (a digital one has the added benefit of being mobile and easily sharable). As we assign vocabulary and students find words new to them in their reading, they add the words to their journal, along with images, online video clips, YouTube videos, and quotes from magazine or newspapers articles, favorite books, interviews, brochures, pamphlets, or any other printed resource that define the word. This journal is not a scrapbook; it's a tool to help students write their own definitions. Here are the instructions I give:

> In your interactive vocabulary journal (IVJ), create a definition for each word. Each definition should be brief and concise and descriptive so that anyone who reads it will understand. The definition should blend a verbal statement with teacher-approved context clues and illustrative resources: images, text excerpts, social media, apps, videos, etc. You will share your IVJ entries with your class.
>
> The journal can also be used to help students understand concepts. Teachers in one school district used it to reinforce literary concepts such as plot, character, conflict, setting, theme, and irony: students wrote their own definitions of the target terms, using information taken from class activities, photographs, music, articles, videos, etc. (Chadwick 2012, 15)

It's often useful to provide guiding questions when using the vocabulary journal to tackle larger concepts. For example, while working with some ELA and social studies teachers on the theme of civil rights, I gave students these questions:

- Can a person, event, or moment justify violence to effect change?
- Should, a person, event, or moment justify violence to effect change?
- Is any region, country, or nation free from discrimination?

Used this way, the journal is a cumulative, sustained learning pathway that allows students to work with concepts, ideas, resources, and tools with which they are familiar, thereby providing ownership and enhancing their comprehension.

Link Literature to Students' Worlds

Tool 1:
The Student Survey,
Appendix A

My remedial tenth graders were reading at eighth-grade level or below. I wanted to teach the literature listed in the curriculum—Edgar Allan Poe, Langston Hughes, Shakespeare—but I knew I couldn't just assign and discuss it. I needed to scaffold and guide my students through the literary terrain. I loved them; I respected them; I learned so much from them. And I knew I had to answer their why questions. Why would I ask them to read works that to them were so very foreign—in language, in character, in setting, in conflict—with no relevance they could readily see? Why on earth were they reading them?

These students were more outspoken than my other classes, I think because they felt so much out of the norm as they understood it. During my first year with them, Carolyn looked up from her textbook as I was reading Poe's "The Raven" aloud. Raising her hand, she said, "Miss, I don't get this. And I don't get why you are making us read it. Who cares about a bird?" As I was formulating a response, Eugene joined in: "Yes, Miss, this stuff don't make no sense." I looked into a sea of faces awaiting a response that would not pay lip service (it's great literature, or it'll be referred to in college) but would provide a reason, a clear rationale they could understand and buy into. I decided to ask, "What kind of stories and poems would you like to read?" In response I got, "Real stuff." "Life." "Nuthin'." When I told them that reading would help them not only in their schoolwork and in passing state assessments but also in life, they stared at me in polite silence. I needed to do something to help them.

The chair of my department, Judith A. Purvis, accepted my proposal to go "off curriculum" for a while, then try to get back on later in the year. With her and the rest of the department's support, I ordered class sets of contemporary books, along with a series of films these students would find interesting—*To Sir, with Love*; *Flowers for Algernon*; *The Outsiders*; *A Tree Grows in Brooklyn*. I also photocopied short stories from Nathaniel Hawthorne's *Tanglewood Tales* and *A Wonder-Book for Girls and Boys*. It worked. We read together, aloud and silently, in one giant reading circle. At first, they were calmer, no heads on desks, no audible sighs of boredom, but still there was no conversation. But as the semester progressed, they began to ask a question or two or three, and I nearly levitated when they laughed at some of situations in the Hawthorne tales. Their sense of disconnection, their default position of derision, faded away.

Interspersing curriculum texts with our off-curriculum ones remained a challenge. They still groaned at Poe's "The Tell-Tale Heart" but were no longer afraid of it (that the story focuses on murder and mayhem helped!). They weren't masterful readers at the end of the semester, but they left the class less resistant to reading and not as defeated by the attempt. (I know because they and their parents told me so.) One year cannot bring about the degree of change we know our students require, but if we mute the outside cacophony as best we can, we can make a significant dent.

In the succeeding years, I've learned that proactively asking for students' input about our subject matter and our work together is not just an eye-opening experience but a necessary component in planning my work, and I developed the survey in Appendix A. (Tailoring it to your specific needs makes it even more effective.) The responses I get amaze and surprise me. Although the survey changes over time, its two basic components—objective and subjective questions—remain constant. I want to know how my students are feeling, how they are thinking, and how they perceive what they are learning. Conducting a survey like this early in the academic year gives us immediate information that informs how we approach the assigned literature and alerts us to potential impediments—reading reticence, vocabulary issues, sensitive topics—we can proactively address. Basic questions include:

- What texts have you read in school recently?
- How often do you read assigned texts completely? Why or why not?
- Do you ever turn to other resources, such as CliffsNotes or online summaries, instead of reading the assigned texts? Why or why not?
- Do you use the skills taught in your English classes beyond those classes? If so, how?
- What are your opinions about the literature you've read in your English classes?
- What do you read outside school?

When I administer a survey of this kind, I ask students to keep their responses anonymous. This engenders honesty and results in a more reflective and honest instructional tool.

John and I have also collaborated on an idea we call "backing into the classics." One day John suggested, "You're going to teach *The Iliad* and *The Odyssey* tomorrow. Have you ever considered how much Clint Eastwood's film *The Unforgiven* parallels Greek tragedy and the classics?" I was initially aghast. Westerns, cowboys, saloons, best-pal horses, and wild shoot-outs linked to the masterpieces of Greek literature? Really!

But he convinced me to rent *The Unforgiven*, watch it, and think about the similarities with some of the Greek classics I so respected. As the stark drama unfolded, I began to open my mind to the film. I saw the parallels; I began to think beyond the text, which in turn, allowed me to imagine other learning pathways by which students could enter assigned texts. Would they learn from this approach? Would it help bring them closer to the classics? My experience has shown they do and it does, because it frames literature from another time in a way today's students can understand and identify with. Tim Rollins' approach of using art instruction and creation—individual and collaborative creation—with the requirement of reading classical and modern literature and informational texts further illustrates this instructional learning pathway. Backing into the classics continues to inform my teaching and my interaction with students.

Tool 2:
Student Journals

Give Students Opportunities to Wrestle with Big Ideas in Literature on Their Own

Although our goals for reading literature with students include helping them recognize timeless themes, they often don't see the connections we do. The most direct way to address these themes is to state them outright, but that approach is typically met with apathy and glazed eyes, not life-changing, rapturous revelations. If we want students to feel the magic of these texts, they must have their own aha! moments. We cannot manufacture these flashes of inspiration, but we can provide favorable conditions in which they can happen.

A structured journal—either digital or on paper—is a place where students can try on ideas, make connections, and consider differing perspectives. I model this learning pathway both digitally and on paper—jotting notes, ideas, observations, questions, even if at the moment, I might not see an immediate use. For example, if you and your class are exploring the idea of free will in the context of race and gender, you might ask students to:

- search both assigned texts and additional texts of their choice (literary, informational, multimedia) for quotes, images, and/or lyrics that pertain to freedom to choose and add them to their journals.
- explain in the journal what made each example of choice and the free will to exercise that choice interesting.
- use the journal to respond to their or your guiding questions about the theme.

Examples of guiding questions pertaining to freedom to choose include:

- How do we exert the freedom to choose in everyday life—at home, in school, with friends, with family?
- Do we ever feel our freedom to choose compromised or nonexistent? Are race and gender a factor in freedom to choose?
- Has the freedom to choose shaped America's definition and image of itself?
- What is free will to you within your community, your culture, your country, and the world?

For students to see the message of a text as meaningful, they must forge their own connections to it. When their connections are not the same as ours (even, perhaps especially, if our connections seem richer and better informed), we can honor their connections initially and use what we learn from their responses to consider how best to approach the text as we continue reading. Our goal is to give students a space of their own to try out ideas together, not create a cumbersome assignment that yields a "correct" interpretation.

| Tool 3:
Collaborative Learning
Communities | Give Students Opportunities to Wrestle with Big Ideas in Literature with Their Peers |

Give Students Opportunities to Wrestle with Big Ideas in Literature with Their Peers

Group work has always held a place in all content areas. In the classes I taught and in the classrooms I work with now, I use collaborative learning communities (CLCs) as the structure for our group work.

ELA educators have honed group interaction to include peer groups for writing and review and Socratic, or inquiry, groups for discussion and critical inquiry and a variety of reading groups. Researchers such as Grant Wiggins, Jay McTighe, Ralph Tyler, Julie Young, Jonathan C. Erwin, and Robert Marzano support the grouping concept. Langer's study (2000) focuses on the efficacy of the small group:

> Group discussions where students had opportunities to discuss their questions and predictions also served to support envisionment building. Sometimes these discussions focused on a topic the teacher had set, but most often they were used as opportunities for the students to discuss the predictions they had written in their journals, the questions they had that they felt they needed to discuss, or an issue related to their reading they thought would be interesting for the small group. It was these small groups that often decided what topics or concerns should then be brought to the whole class for discussion. One student in one eleventh-grade suburban class said: "When we have our discussions we learn a lot from each other. We can really give each other ideas. It's not just one person's ideas, it's all of them put together." (24)

With grouping students, there is always the nagging concern with how and whom to group. In my early years of teaching, I always formed the groups, but as I listened to and observed my students, I found I could use the reading survey and writing sample with which I began the semester to form groups based on:

- diversity—class, ethnicity, and any other demographics I am able to glean that prompt a mixture of student voices
- a range of reading levels
- a range of work ethics.

Students don't use these criteria to form groups; they seek out likeness, sameness. My concept of the purpose of grouping reflects Dewey's description (1916) of the natural proclivity

THE POWER OF LEARNING WITHOUT
A "CORRECT" ANSWER

───────────── ■ ─────────────

True literacy requires empathy: placing oneself in a new context and understanding a contrary viewpoint. Literature, in particular literature that addresses issues of gender, class, and race, provides students with a bridge to literacy skills. In my fourteen years teaching secondary English, three American novels (The Great Gatsby, Adventures of Huckleberry Finn, *and* Their Eyes Were Watching God) *consistently resonated with my students, prompting passionate and articulate responses.*

In Zora Neale Hurston's Their Eyes Were Watching God, *Jody's abuse of Janie and her decision to stay with him are troublesome. My students encountered a beautiful, wise, and strong heroine making an apparently weak decision. How could she do this?! Discussion was fierce. No other moment generated such heated debate. Students struggled with themselves and one another to articulate their emotions and ideas. We wrote, we processed, we sat in silence, we argued. Like many discussions worth having, it left us asking more questions, seeking answers where perhaps there were none.*

—Holly E. Parker, University of New England; ELA teacher (January 14, 2015)

of grouping as early as kindergarten: It is not enough that the circle is a convenient way of grouping the children. It must be used "because it is a symbol of the collective life of mankind in general (141)."

Using this predilection to accomplish the instructional aims that grouping is meant to achieve—collaboration, discovery, exploration, emergence and privilege of voice, responsibility, and consequence—is well worth the time and effort it takes to compose them deliberately and carefully. And if some blends don't work, they are easily changed.

A blend of abilities is most often the aim of grouping because strong students will help less able students and eager and loquacious students will draw out those who are reticent. However, students who are eager, strong, and loquacious often dominate the quieter, less aggressive students, even if the quieter students are amazing thinkers. But if we reshuffle the composition of the groups, we break up any cohesion and coherence the group may have initiated.

One class of juniors asked if they could please remain in their original groups; they even wanted their desks to remain in group formation whether they were doing group work or not. I agreed. As students in my other classes heard about our little experiment, they asked whether they could do the same. We had to leave notes, asking the maintenance crews not to return the desks to the traditional formation. Much to our unanticipated surprise, my students and I found we were unintentionally developing small learning communities. Over time, even the more reticent and less able students become engaged. This small start had a significant ripple effect in my instructional perspective and how I think about differentiated learning pathways and literacy learning.

I continued this type of sustained grouping in my university instruction, but not until I was part of a group collaboration with educators of diverse backgrounds did I fully understand the instructional implications and potential. Our aim was to reflect, rethink, and design instructional approaches for secondary students that would engage them in ways conducive to who they are, taking into account ethnicity, gender, class, and region but not to the extent that we would sacrifice rigor and expectations. It soon became apparent that the act of working as a group was key to achieving these goals. In *Socratic Seminars and Literature Circles for Middle and High School English* (2001), Moeller and Moeller maintain:

> By giving students the opportunity and practice of setting up their own readings, they take ownership of reading. With practice and repetition, it may continue even after they leave school. Second, choice is an integral part of literate behavior. Being forced to read too often results in not reading at all—even when one has the freedom to do so. (181)

Informed by the traditional concept of grouping and sparked by new generations of students, our vision of CLCs has several key building blocks:

- *Setting.* The instructional aim of the CLC allows for and encourages a number of social surroundings, a shared cultural outlook, and even class for collaborative work, inside and outside of class.
- *Atmosphere.* Establishing a physical location in the classroom and an atmosphere conducive to reassurance and support, of listening to and learning from one another is critical for the CLCs to function effectively.
- *Surroundings.* Each CLC exists with a virtual sea of CLCs in the classroom, where teachers blend in and out—sometimes noticed, sometimes not. At the core of the CLC activities is literature that pulls members from their present, their time and space, their culture and ethnicity, and allows them to work together and separately as they explore time and peoples they may never physically encounter.

Twenty-first-century students require that we rethink the group—its formation, its setting, its immediate aim, its ultimate learning objective(s). For these students, technology, organic adaptability, and sustainability are critical aspects of sustaining the collaborative process.

While traditional grouping is traditionally random and not necessarily sustained, CLCs are sustained throughout the academic year and comprise the same students, who form a bond of collaboration, trust, and sharing and develop a cumulative learning style and work repertoire. Working with assigned literary texts, CLCs may also draw on video, animation, music, graphics, informational texts, oral histories, and interviews. CLCs offer opportunities for ELA and cross-curricular texts and ideas to meet and blend. This instructional pathway encourages each student in the CLC to develop unique ways of inquiry and analysis and evaluation—individually and collaboratively—thereby enriching her or his learning experience inside and outside the class-room. Students not only take on guiding questions while writing independently in their journals but also address new issues and concerns they discover while working within the CLC.

CLCs in no way detract from teacher guidance and individual student initiative; rather, students move back and forth between independent work and collaboration, and teachers' instructional roles become even more critical. With the CLC approach, ELA teachers guide and facilitate. More important, we privilege each student's voice and perspective in addition to the group's perspective—even if that perspective isn't what we anticipate or something with which we agree. We are not the omniscient presence; instead, we, too, are learners and discoverers with our students, an instructional relationship William James, John Dewey, and Paulo Freire support and encourage. Working with these groups, I have learned so much from their conversations, their debates, and most of all their questions. My presence is neither the focus nor a potential impediment to their voice. I often have the opportunity to ask questions that prompt further conversation.

The CLC learning approach also gives students opportunities to develop their research skills and the confidence to rely on their ability to think critically. Each student contributes to the group's efforts to read the assigned text and to broaden their comprehension of it in the context of inferential implications. Students are encouraged to share information in their journals or literary analysis rubrics (discussed in Chapter 4). Here, too, students may pose questions to and/or engage in dialogue with their teacher. They can expand these conversations and explorations in chat rooms and other social media. The CLC approach reflects how students gather and understand information today. They no longer see the assigned literary text as daunting or as unassailable. In a very real sense, the perceived challenges and breadth of work by Shakespeare, Faulkner, Morrison, Blake, Ortiz Cofer, Neruda, Homer, or Tennyson, for example, are less overwhelming, less frightening.

The initial aim of the CLC concept is to germinate inquiry, discussion, and exploration; an additional aim is to encourage students to share their work, either with the class or the school or in the surrounding community through projects guided by their teacher. The CLC allows students to leverage the technology and interests they have and drill more deeply into an assigned literary text. Their approaches will vary, and they have the opportunity to describe why they chose their approach, what they learned by using these elements, and what this learning means to them.

Don't Let Students Excuse Themselves from the Work

As we celebrate critical thinking in our students, it's not unusual to find—sometimes in our brightest students—attempts to use critical thinking as an excuse for not fully engaging in the work. When I was invited to conduct classes at Richardson High School (Texas), I encountered two young men who so didn't want to read, who felt so disconnected from the text that they decided to find a way to cancel the assignment. One morning one of them handed me his KKK membership card, the implication—threat perhaps?—being that he would not be participating in our work that day. The other young man, in another class, refused to read *The Adventures of Tom Sawyer* and *Adventures of Huckleberry Finn* because he objected to a white man's writing about slavery. He asked to be excused from class and all assignments for the week.

The student with the KKK membership card perhaps expected to be removed from class for threatening or intimidating a teacher; at the very least he assumed I would overlook his failure to participate. The student who claimed offense at Twain's writing about slavery thought he would not be required to do any work at all. However, if we sidestep the false choices students like these present, we can still engage them. The most fruitful path is to acknowledge the student's concern and treat it as valid (even when we suspect an ulterior motive) but not let that get in the way of our learning goals.

I read the first student's card, smiled, and said, "Thank you." When the other teachers asked what he had given to me, I showed them. They were aghast and wondered whether we could proceed with the class. We did, and I made a point of asking the young man questions about the assigned texts. Knowing and monitoring my audience and working collaboratively with the students was essential. Maintaining my focus on the texts and my instructional aims piqued students' curiosity, and the literature provided a vehicle to explore that curiosity.

I asked the department chair and the sophomore/junior ELA teachers if I could assign the other young man Frances Ellen Watkins Harper's *Iola Leroy*, or *Shadows Uplifted* (1892) instead. He requested that he be allowed to do his reading in the library, but I insisted he remain in class and add to our conversation and explorations with his perceptions about a contemporary African American woman writing about slavery. (It quickly became clear that he didn't want to read anything, whatever the ethnicity of a book's author.)

In both instances, what could have resulted in a nonlearning, even counterproductive, moment resulted in teachable moments. The other students in the class did learn; they did ask questions; they did respond to my questions. And most of them lingered after each of those class periods or returned to me at the end of the day to ask more questions—including the young man who gave me his KKK card. I often ask myself, "So, Jocelyn, what I have learned?" With my Irving High students and with students around the country, I have learned that our ability to read our students as audience, maintain our expectations, and adjust instructional approaches and tools facilitates literacy learning based on literature.

FRAMING OUR EXPECTATIONS IN RELEVANCE

Our expectations for all of our students must be to facilitate and provide learning opportunities—learning opportunities that are not necessarily easy, not endlessly fun, not without rigor, but always filled with unexpected discovery and exploration and most of all curiosity.

The tools and strategies in this chapter represent instructional learning pathways that in turn represent our twenty-first-century students, also known as Generation Z (see "Anatole 2013,

Kingston 2014, Levit 2015, Raphelson 2014, Wallop 2014, Tulgan and RainmakerThinking 2013). Because these students make meaning differently in so many ways not only because of when they were born but also because of technological, social, and economic developments and the tsunami of social media, we, too, must adjust—not only our expectations for them and the role of literature but also how we construct the instructional pathways to achieve our expectations. Our ability to make our literature relevant and, therefore, necessary, lies in communicating and illustrating how our students' concerns and challenges and aspirations are reflected in the texts. The vehicles through which we can ignite our students' connections are instructional approaches that resonate with their world.

> Past experiences always influence new learning. Not all of our students come from a language-rich reading/learning environment. Some of them are more Huckleberry Finn than Tom Sawyer. They rarely miss school because school is warm on a cold winter day, and breakfast and lunch are served. School is a safe, predictable environment. In a home environment where academic success is not valued and reading is not encouraged, it is difficult for students to become engaged in the learning experience and have the desire to read and be successful. [Many of our students are fortunate.] They are active students and provide strong modeling for the less fortunate ones. Their peers' academic motivation and their school's culture are influencing factors. The perceptions of friends' academic values affect the way they approach reading and the learning situation. (Ramah Troutman, ELA teacher, personal communication, February 3, 2015)

Thinking Outside the Box

3

EMBRACING INFORMATIONAL TEXTS IN LITERATURE CLASSROOMS

For we believe that a paper devoted to the dissemination of useful knowledge among our brethren, and to their moral and religious improvement, must meet with the cordial approbation of every friend to humanity. . . . We form a spoke in the human wheel, and it is necessary that we should understand our dependence on the different parts, and theirs on us, in order to perform our part with propriety. . . . The civil rights of a people being of the greatest value, it shall ever be our duty to vindicate our brethren, when oppressed, and to lay the case before the publick.

—Samuel E. Cornish and John B. Russwurm, "To Our Patrons," *Freedom's Journal,* 1827

■

In the area of comprehension, television has turned an active function of the mind (reading) into a passive one (viewing). The lost component is imagination. If one reads *Orange Is the New Black,* for example, one has to imagine the environment and the inmates. In the television version, all is laid out before the viewer. At the same time, television has expanded our ability to comprehend the world through images and sound. Reading a politician's statement in a newspaper and seeing that politician making the same statement at a televised news conference may lead one to vastly different conclusions. The tone of voice, facial expressions, and body language all contribute to what might be called "visual literacy."

—Hal Gessner, CBS News Productions, New York (personal communication, December 21, 2014)

■

It is a cliché to say that the Internet is "just a tool." It's not. It is a living force and phenomenon that can be read and used with the same passion as one should read and use Homer's *The Odyssey* in the living of one's daily life.

—Tim Rollins, artist and educator (personal communication, January 29, 2015)

Q UITE RECENTLY, I WAS ASKED TO TALK about and introduce *Narrative of the Life of Frederick Douglass* to a class of high school boys at Woodberry Forest School, in Virginia. However, I can never focus on a single author in isolation—one cannot discuss any text, particularly a personal narrative or an autobiography, without exploring the period, the literature, the concerns, and the people who might have had some impact on the writing. So I decided to include complementary texts, events, and people that affected Douglass and discuss them in light of his personal narrative.

In addition, I had to think about my audience—high school boys—and the school's classical instructional approach. To complement, even clarify, Douglass' personal narrative, I included one primary example from *Douglass' Monthly*, a journal he published from 1858–1863; a primary source example of *Freedom's Journal*, an excerpt from Elizabeth Cady Stanton (1827), and excerpts from Emerson's "The American Scholar" and "Self-Reliance." My rationale for blending these specific texts was that Douglass' narrative is at once autobiography and slave narrative and American success metaphor.

But who was this man—what inspired him to act, to be an activist, to refuse to give up in the face of seeming and real insurmountable challenges, especially at a time in U.S. history when the country itself was groaning, stretching, and careening into a spasm that would literally break apart the country and its people? My instructional goal was to bring this scene, this moment, to the students, using these blended texts—both literary and nonfiction/informational. I hoped that by experiencing them, the students would have questions, would be curious, and would want to know more—enough to read the autobiography in its entirety. It was an amazing experience for me, for the students, and for their teacher.

As we sat in a circle, I asked:

Me: *So what is your initial impression of Frederick Douglass?*

Student 1: *Well, he had a hard time and escaped from slavery.*

Student 2: *He was unique, right, because he could read and write and was a slave?*

Student 3: *I really like him.*

The remaining comments conveyed similar sentiments. My students at Irving High School in the late 1970s and early 1980s offered similar responses at the beginning of the year, as do the students I encounter throughout the country today. This reticence is partly because I am new to their classroom; it also stems from the way students and many adults read in the twenty-first century—scanning, taking the text in chunks, instead of experiencing it. (Henry James, who advised readers to engage a text, particularly his own, in little bits, would be shocked and dismayed.)

I then asked the students what else they knew about this period in American literary history. Again, there were very few direct responses. I assured them I was not there to test them, there were no wrong responses; I was just curious. Next, I began building up to the narrative, setting the scene: "Let's take a look at what was surrounding Douglass—events, people, issues in America that would affect him and his views and actions. I want to ask you a question, and you will have to guess the answer. When was the first African American newspaper published?"

Student responses included the 1970s, 1960s, 1980s, 1950s, 1930s. They were all surprised when I said 1827 and shared a primary source example. What happened next is exactly how I wanted the learning process to proceed:

> Student 1: *Wow! Why? Why did they publish? What did they publish?*
>
> Student 2: *What was their goal?*
>
> Student 3: *Who read this newspaper?*
>
> Student 4: *How did they distribute it, and were there any other African American newspapers?*

The increase in the students' interest was clear. They even sat up a bit straighter and leaned in to the growing conversation.

Next, I showed them two primary sources—the first edition of *Freedom's Journal* and an edition of *Douglass' Monthly* (see Figure 3.1). As each student viewed the documents (one they could hold in their hands, the other they could see on my iPad), I was thrilled to see that they were actually reading the texts and that their reading prompted further questions about Frederick Douglass.

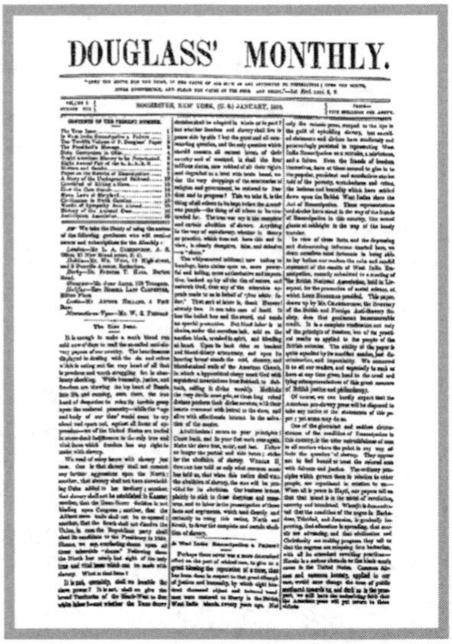
DOUGLASS' MONTHLY.

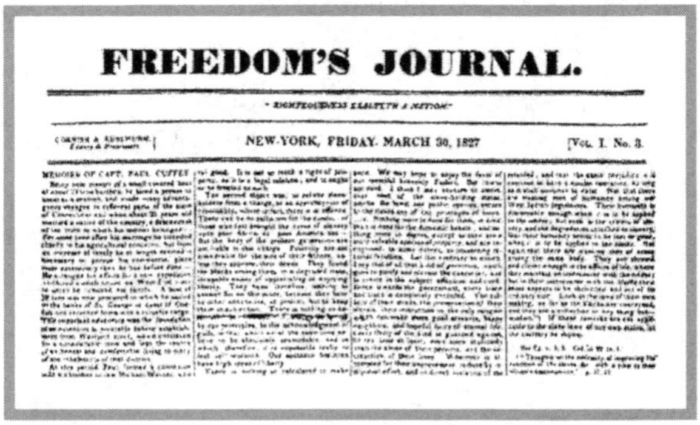
FREEDOM'S JOURNAL.

NEW-YORK, FRIDAY, MARCH 30, 1827

Vol. I. No. 3.

Figure 3.1

Students' curiosity was piqued when they had an opportunity to review the earliest African American newspapers.

I mentioned the relationship of Emerson's essays to the unique "Americanness" of Douglass' language and style in his *Narrative*. Before we realized it, the period ended, with everyone still in animated conversation—a very different response from that at the beginning of the class.

INFORMATIONAL TEXTS AND THE COMMON CORE

The Common Core bases its focus on informational and complex texts on research reported by the National Assessment of Educational Progress:

> *The Standards aim to align instruction with this framework so that many more students than at present can meet the requirements of college and career readiness. In K–5, the Standards follow NAEP [National Assessment of Educational Progress]'s lead in balancing the reading of literature with the reading*

of informational texts, including texts in history/social studies, science, and technical subjects. . . . Fulfilling the Standards for 6–12 ELA requires much greater attention to a specific category of informational text—literary nonfiction—than has been traditional. (Common Core State Standards Initiative 2015b)

The authors of the Common Core also suggest that familiarity with informational text is an additional step in building knowledge:

Students must be immersed in information about the world around them if they are to develop the strong general knowledge and vocabulary they need to become successful readers and be prepared for college, career, and life. Informational texts play an important part in building students' content knowledge. Further, it is vital for students to have extensive opportunities to build knowledge through texts so they can learn independently. (Common Core State Standards Initiative 2015c)

Although nonfiction/informational texts have always had a significant presence in ELA classrooms, the Common Core's increased focus has generated opposing views about whether ELA instruction benefits from their inclusion.

Opponent Betsy Woodruff (2012), a William F. Buckley Fellow at the National Review Institute, cites the potential of political intrusion:

The Common Core State Standards look to balance literary reading with the reading of informational texts, including texts in history, the social sciences, natural sciences, and technical subjects, according to a document [http://www.corestandards.org/assets/CCSSI_ELA%20Standards.pdf] from the standards' creators. (Stanley Kurtz has explained [http://www.nationalreview.com/corner/334878/obama-and-your -childs-mind-stanley-kurtz] how this could enable the federal government to use classrooms to proselytize students to adopt its political goals.)

Sandra Stotsky (2012) warns that focusing on informational texts would result in a "devastating impact on literary study and critical thinking" (1). She further asserts that "the decline in readiness for college reading [since the 1960s] stems in large part from an increasingly incoherent, less challenging literature curriculum. . . . This decline has been propelled by the fragmentation of the year-long English course into semester electives, the conversion of junior high schools, and the assignment of easier, shorter, and contemporary texts—often in the name of multiculturalism" (1–2). Opponents concur that ultimately informational texts will not allow students "to benefit intellectually" (Solochek, Fitzpatrick, and Sherman 2013).

Supporter Kelly Gallagher, an ELA teacher at Magnolia High School, in Anaheim, California, views the informational texts he presently uses in his classrooms as instructional vehicles, or pathways, into literature: "I am dealing with kids who are just as smart as kids always have been, but they're coming to me with much narrower prior knowledge and understanding of the world. You have to know things to read things" (Gewertz 2012, 23). Doug Lemov, author of *Teach Like a Champion* and managing director of Uncommon Schools, a charter system in Rochester and Troy, New York, also views informational texts as a means of addressing what he describes as "one of the biggest barriers to reading success and comprehension . . . the knowledge deficit. . . . Reading the same thing multiple times is good. Prereading is good. Reading multiple texts is good. The best 'prereading' . . . is reading" (Gewertz 2012, 23).

I find these conversations and debates both illustrative and unsettling. Celebrating Women's History Month, March 21, 2014, Pioneer Institute sponsored a forum, focusing on women's roles and place. Participating along with Catherine Clinton, Sandra Stotsky, and Joan Hendrick in a panel session titled "Remember the Ladies: Women in U.S. History, Literature, and Schooling," I was pleased and energized when the 350 attendees (teachers and others interested in K–12 education) asked probing, reflective questions about women's representation in the quilt of literacy learning. At the same time, I was dismayed by some of the evident misinformation, not only about literature but also about the "place" of informational texts in our nation's classrooms. For example, no one questioned why we teach Emily Dickinson's poetry, but many were surprised to learn that we also teach Margaret Fuller's essays, Sojourner Truth's speech "Ain't I a Woman?" and the "Declaration of Sentiments" presented at the convention on women's rights held in Seneca Falls, New York, in 1848. Why were they so surprised?

To those of us who have always used informational texts to enhance, illustrate, and contextualize literature, this pedagogical divide seems discordant. I cannot effectively teach *Adventures of Huckleberry Finn* without relying on informational texts to frame the reading and exploration for twenty-first-century students. As students read "Huck," and encounter such words/phrases such as *bill of sale* and *runaway slave notice* that to them are completely foreign, I provide illustrative informational documents and notices in contemporary periodicals (see Figure 3.2). Capturing their curiosity, I generate more interest in their reading the Twain book and asking even more questions.

Teaching any Edgar Allan Poe poem or short story without including excerpts from his engaging

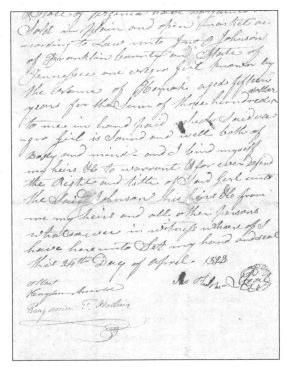

Figure 3.2
A Bill of Sale for Hannah, a Fifteen-Year-Old Girl

and instructive essay "Philosophy of Composition" deprives students of a window into an artist's mind: how does an artist choose an emblem or symbol? Choose colors, or words, or images? Think about the message and the audience? Pairing a Poe literary selection with this essay not only contextualizes the work but also enables students to establish their own relationship with Poe. Experiencing him from a different perspective, they discover, much to their surprise and joy, that Poe had to think about and wrestle with his writing just as they do! They begin to explore, discover, think about, and understand how this "weird" nineteenth-century writer, whom they love to be frightened by, is still relevant today—not only his themes but also his ideas about communication, critical thinking, and the craft of writing. Edgar Allan Poe begins to speak to them.

Texts that may initially be assumed to be uninteresting to our twenty-first-century students, such as *The Tragedy of Julius Caesar*, *The Scarlet Letter*, *Joy Luck Club*, or *Invisible Man*, may create quite a different experience when paired with a piece of nonfiction/informational text, thereby making both genres not only clearer, but more important, engaging, and interesting.

Fountas and Pinnell (2006), in *Teaching for Comprehending and Fluency*, also emphasize the importance of blending a variety of textual formats, including informational texts, to provide students a variety of pathways into literacy: "For readers to build effective and flexible literacy processing systems, the texts they encounter in their literacy education must be varied, well written, accessible, and plentiful" (123). This blending takes students on journeys "within, beyond, and about the text" (32). Nonfiction/informational texts can allow, even encourage, students to (1) "think within the text," (2) "think beyond the text," and (3) "think about the text" (172–77). Although their book concentrates on grades K–8, their pedagogical philosophy is sound for grades 9–12 as well, for our instructional goal is the same: using literature to engage students and hone their communication and critical thinking skills.

For those not teaching ELA, the dichotomy is more pronounced. In November 2012, I participated in a NCTE panel on James Baldwin's fiction and nonfiction/informational essays and afterward contributed to a *New York Times* article on the same subject (Lee 2014). Questions raised by attendees and readers revealed just how much confusion exists with regard to two separate yet related questions: Do ELA classes still teach informational/nonfiction texts? Did ELA classes ever teach informational/nonfiction texts? What defines an informational text?

Judging from my experiences and conversations, I'm pretty sure preservice and practicing teachers, parents, and especially our students wonder just what constitutes informational text. To address this question, we begin where all English language arts teachers love to commence a search—with a trusted resource. I have often wondered where we would be without the Oxford English Dictionary, or the OED.

The phrase *informational text* does not appear in the dictionary, but it does cite the term *informational* from the *Education Research Bulletin*: "Two types of reading are generally recognized today [1927], the informational or work type and the recreatory [sic] or leisure type." Looking up *nonfiction*, however, we find: "[first used in 1867] prose writing other than fiction, such as history, biography, and reference works, esp. that which is concerned with the narrative depiction of factual events; the genre comprising this." These citations clarify what defines and describes nonfiction texts often used in ELA classrooms, such as William Wordsworth's "Preface to Lyrical Ballads" or *The Diary of a Young Girl*. But how and when did the way we use nonfiction in our classrooms become synonymous with the way we use informational text?

"Information Literacy: A Literature Review" (Rader 2000), a brief but concise and informative review of informational literacy published by Manchester Metropolitan University, spans its conscious development from 1973–2003. By 1994 three studies in particular—by H. Rader, C. S. Doyle, and C. S. Bruce, who build on one another's research, as well as that by others—compile working definitions and criteria delineating informational literacy. The following excerpt correlates in many ways with how we currently view and teach both literature and nonfiction/informational text:

> *…an information literate person combines the following qualities and abilities:*
>
> 1) has values which promote information use
> 2) has knowledge of the world of information
> 3) recognises that accurate information is a basis for intelligent decision making
> 4) recognises the need for information
> 5) formulates questions based on that need
> 6) identifies potential and appropriate sources of information
> 7) develops successful search strategies
> 8) accesses a wide range of sources of information, including computer-based and other technologies
> 9) evaluates information during all phases of information problem solving
> 10) organises information for practical application
> 11) integrates new information into an existing body of knowledge
> 12) uses critical thinking in information problem solving
> 13) approaches information problem solving in a dynamic and reflective manner
> 14) engages in independent, self-directed learning
> 15) considers the information needs of others when communicating. (6–7)

Although the majority of these criteria are facets of ELA related to critical writing, critical thinking, and critical listening and speaking, 3, 6, 10, 11,12, 13, and 14 speak to our goals as we teach literature. From this perspective, the essays, diaries, biographies, journals, reports, speeches, and articles with which we complement our literary texts meet many of the criteria for informational texts.

The familiar nonfiction we have referenced in the past—the brief bits of letters in our literature anthologies or the historical documents that are part of our American and world literature curricula—retains its importance to fiction. We now need to be able to recognize unfamiliar nonfiction, even types that are not solely text, such as lyrics, graphic novels, film, television, documentaries. Our task is to find texts, of whatever type, that provide a richer, illustrative background, as well as have contemporary relevance for our students.

WHAT DOES USING INFORMATIONAL TEXTS IN THE LITERATURE CLASSROOM LOOK LIKE?

During a National Council of Teachers of English convention in 2009, many teachers listened to Carol Jago describe and recommend some informational texts we could use in our classes to add another dimension to literature. I have found not only her specific recommendations spot on, but also I was already a convert to this instructional strategy. My students, at both high school and graduate levels, responded well to this learning pathway. While I have since used all the titles Jago recommended with students and teachers, one title, *Outbreak*, by Bryn Barnard, I found immediately useful. Nonfiction works provide context and clarity within a literary/historical timeline, but teaching Defoe's *Journal of the Plague Year* or Pepys' *Diary* entries about the plague to readers of varied ability, even graduate students, was often daunting. The picture book *Outbreak* grabbed the attention of my students and made them want to explore the more difficult ones. Including *Outbreak* created an additional learning pathway, filling in and informing students without threatening them. (See Figure 3.3.)

The specific fiction and nonfiction/informational texts we blend into ELA instruction require a sound rationale. Allowing students to explore Emerson's informational speech (and subsequent essay) "The American Scholar," for example, enables them to understand more clearly the nineteenth-century desire to blend American literature with the emerging vision America espoused politically and socially. Walt Whitman, Edgar Allan Poe, Countee Cullen, Lorraine Hansberry, Richard Wright, Sherman Alexie, and so many others whose works we teach take on a different meaning, relevance, and import for students when we include appropriate nonfiction/informational texts aligned with them.

When I taught eleventh-grade American literature, my department often relied on nonfiction/informational texts to complement the literature. Although we grounded our approach in the literature of the period, we recognized that our students would better understand and experience the

Figure 3.3

Using complimentary texts made Defoe and Pepys less daunting for students.

period if we included nonfiction/informational texts that positioned the literature within a real context. Here are the nonfiction/informational texts we used for this unit and the literary works to which we connected the texts:

Informational Texts

Douglass: "Our Paper and Its Prospects," *The North Star* *(December 3, 1847)*

This riveting but seldom assigned statement from Douglass' antislavery newspaper adds a new dimension to all of the literature of this period. From the article:

> It is neither a reflection on the fidelity, nor a disparagement of the ability of our friends and fellow-laborers, to assert what "common sense affirms and only folly denies," that the man who has suffered the wrong is the man to demand redress—that the man STRUCK is the man to CRY OUT—and that he who has endured the cruel pangs of Slavery is the man to advocate Liberty. It is evident we must be our own representatives and advocates, not exclusively, but peculiarly—not distinct from, but in connection with our white friends. In the grand struggle for liberty and equality now waging, it is meet, right, and essential that there should arise in our ranks authors and editors, as well as orators, for it is in these capacities that the most permanent good can be rendered to our cause.

Emerson: "The American Scholar"

This essay permeates this unit because of Emerson's theme regarding the necessity and subsequent search for an authentic American voice, "an American scholar." Therefore, references and reflections on this essay will occur with each literary selection.

Poe: "Philosophy of Composition"

This essay takes readers directly into the creative and rhetorical mind of the artist—the poet—Poe. The artist creates a delineated and clear creative road map, revealing process and intent for audience, occasion, purpose. Continuing to examine, compare, and contrast this essay with Poe's poetry enables further drilling and analysis.

Poe: "Review of Hawthorne's Twice-Told Tales"

Poe's review describes and explains the codification and importance of the short story as its own genre—unique to

Figure 3.4
The North Star, Fredrick Douglass' nineteenth-century antislavery newspaper

American letters—again echoing Emerson's call for an authentic American voice. In addition, students can compare and contrast individual and unique styles each writer brings to this new genre.

Emerson: "Self-Reliance"
In this essay (1916) Emerson asserts the importance not only of the individual but also, more importantly, of one's ability to understand oneself and thereby trust oneself to develop a unique voice and perspective. This essay allows readers to experience how literary and nonfiction writers and thinkers of the time embraced and expressed new ideas, styles, and concepts.

LITERARY WORKS

Thoreau: "Walden"

Stowe: *Uncle Tom's Cabin*

Melville: *Billy Budd, Sailor*

Melville: *Moby Dick; or, The Whale*

Poe: "The Raven"

Poe: "To Helen"

Poe: "The Bells"

Emerson: "The Snowstorm"

Emerson: "Concord Hymn"

Poe: "Ligeia"

Poe: "The Masque of the Red Death"

Poe: "The Fall of the House of Usher"

Poe: "The Tell-Tale Heart"

Poe: "The Cask of Amontillado"

Hawthorne: "The Birthmark"

Hawthorne: "Young Goodman Brown"

Hawthorne: "My Kinsman, Major Molineux"

Hawthorne: "Rappiccini's Daughter"

Hawthorne: *The House of the Seven Gables*

Irving: "The Legend of Sleepy Hollow"

Irving: "Rip Van Winkle"

Melville: "Bartleby, the Scrivener"

Hawthorne: *The Scarlet Letter*

The nonfiction/informational texts complement and in some instances clarify the literature. The nonfiction essays contextualize the audience, occasion, and purpose of the literature—its aims, its passions, its style, and its message. But do they help us reach all our goals for students? Do they help students use critical thinking in information problem solving? Do they require the students to work dynamically and reflectively? Do they foster independent, self-directed learning?

What would happen to the students' experience in this unit if we emphasized learning literacy, diversity, and various pathways and resources? To find out, I added the texts in the list that follows to include varied perspectives and equally varied experiences, cultures, and voices to our examination of national literature and American romanticism between 1826 and 1861.

Added Informational Texts

Fuller, ed.: *The Dial: A Magazine for Literature, Philosophy, and Religion*

Russwurm, ed.: *Freedom's Journal* (the first African American newspaper)
These periodicals provide, like "The American Scholar," immersive cultural, economic, social, and political road maps into the conversations, concerns, and issues of the time.

Fuller: "Woman in the Nineteenth Century" (originally entitled "The Great Lawsuit" and considered a revolutionary text for its time)
This essay reflects Fuller's personal growth from feminism to the politics of freedom. In it she argues for women and men to strive for and fulfill their potential—intellectually and spiritually—regardless of gender and other differences.

Truth: "Ain't I a Woman?"
In this pivotal and pointed speech, presented at the 1851 Women's Convention in Akron, Ohio, Sojourner Truth argues for equality regardless of race, gender, and class. She illustrates beyond question the importance of voice and perspective, regardless of class, race, gender, or privilege.

Stanton: "Address to the New York State Legislature"
Addressing the Judiciary Committee of the State Legislature of New York in 1860, Stanton powerfully argues for the rights of women. To illustrate and explicate her claim, she compares the social and political subjugation of women to that of the subjugation of slaves in the South.

Our young people are flooded with academic demands: learn this skill, absorb this content, perform this assessment. Literature can bridge that torrent and allow students to engage, reflect, and develop empathy. Hard literacy skills are indeed vital to effective communication. But literature can give young people something meaningful and insightful to say.

—Holly E. Parker, University of New England; ELA teacher (January 14, 2015)

A WORD ABOUT LETTERS

A recent compilation, Letters of Note: An Eclectic Collection of Correspondence Deserving of an Audience *by Shaun Usher (2014), is an effective and unusual instructional pathway comprising primary source letters dating from BCE to the present. He asserts, "[D]espite their many flavors, I am hopeful that all will captivate you as they have me and whisk you to a point in the time far more effectively than the average history book. Indeed, I can think of no better way to learn about the past than through the often candid correspondence of those who lived it."*

Jacobs: *Incidents in the Life of a Slave Girl*

The slave narrative as a nonfiction literary genre was not only informative during the nineteenth century but also was a vehicle for immediate audience engagement into the reality of being a slave, usually from the male point of view. Jacobs' narrative presents this experience from the perspective of a girl who becomes a woman, longing for freedom, under the yoke of slavery for the first twenty-seven years of her life.

Douglass: *Narrative of the Life of Frederick Douglass*

Audiences thoughout the Northeast heard and read many slave narratives with the aid of the abolitionist movement, but few narratives had the immediate and lasting impact of Douglass'. Differentiating his narrative from most of them was Douglass' rhetorical delivery—organization, language, illustrations, and overall classical style.

Douglass: *What to the Slave Is the Fourth of July?*

A prolific writer and speechmaker, Douglass uses one of the United States' most cherished and celebrated holidays to compare and contrast, define and illustrate, the basic inequity of slavery. He uses the document on which the day focuses, the Constitution of the United States, arguing for "freedom's reign" and "human brotherhood."

Easter Wings *by George Herbert*

Lord, who createdst man in wealth and store,
  Though foolishly he lost the same,
    Decaying more and more,
      Till he became
        Most poore:
          With thee
          O let me rise
        As larks, harmoniously,
      And sing this day thy victories:
Then shall the fall further the flight in me.

My tender age in sorrow did beginner
  And still with sicknesses and shame.
    Thou didst so punish sinne,
      That I became
        Most thinne.
          With thee
          Let me combine,
        And feel thy victorie:
      For, if I imp my wing on thine,
Affliction shall advance the flight in me.

The difference is startling: including texts by women and people of color contributes significantly to increased comprehension and engagement. I have since used this curriculum with students around the country, and it has resulted in engagement, curiosity, critical inquiry, and a desire for further exploration.

Similarly, reading poetry is far more interactive for students when I include nonfiction that lays the writer's process bare, particularly Poe's "Philosophy of Composition." ELA teachers love poetry; our students, many of them, fear it. They don't think about the relationship this genre shares with lyrics they like or rhythms they enjoy. When twelfth graders initially see George Herbert's seventeenth-century poem "Easter Wings" (1633), for example, they do not also think of graffiti or hip-hop.

As students first "see" then read this poem, I refer them to Poe's thoughts regarding audience, occasion, and purpose, as well as "the choice of an impression, or effect, to be conveyed," "the intensity of the intended effect," and "some artistic piquancy which might serve me as a key-note in the construction of the poem, some pivot upon which the whole structure might turn" (1846, 640–44). Thinking about and applying Poe's rationale and process for creating poetry, which he defines, illustrates, and delineates so clearly, students not only begin to understand Poe's poetry but also can better evaluate, experience, and analyze poetry from other periods and cultures outside the nineteenth century. As one of my twelfth graders asked, "Why don't all poets do this so we can get it?

THE BIG PAYOFF: ENGAGED STUDENTS WHO CONNECT WITH LITERATURE

What drives us as ELA teachers and continues to fuel our passion and devotion to our craft and our career is always the "big payoff." Most of us never witness this payoff, for it comes not at the end of each academic year but later—sometimes much later. Our students will take the literature, the conversations, the discovery and explorations, and their ability to question and wrangle with all types of texts, drilling into them, questioning them, analyzing them; our students will use this experience to make informed, critical decisions in everyday life, in college, in the workplace, even in recreation. Our big payoff is instilling, through both literature and nonfiction/informational texts, literacy learning for life. Using informational texts wisely in our classrooms brings us and our students closer to the big payoff. Along the way, we are rewarded with glimpses of the kind of critical thinking and drive we hope our students will carry into their adult lives.

BUT ISN'T THERE A DOWNSIDE?

Embracing informational texts in the ELA classroom wholeheartedly—not just including a few here and there—raises questions. How can we find time to include more texts in our already overcrowded curriculum? Won't including so many informational texts prevent us from focusing deeply on literature? How will including informational texts affect struggling readers and English language learners?

We understandably worry that if we devote more time to nonfiction/informational texts, we may dilute the literature we so love and want to share with our students. In any case, including a variety of informational texts will necessarily take time away from teaching literature.

True, it's not possible to insert more texts into our curriculums, include every piece of literature we want, and continue to teach literature as a series of teacher-directed lectures or close readings. However, if our goal is to help students become independent, critical thinkers, a shift away from teacher-centric instruction is important and necessary. Rather than transmit insights about literature to our students, we need to provide opportunities for them to make their own connections and test their own ideas.

We get a glimpse of what this looks like at Uncommon Schools, in New York, where ELA teachers "assign four or five nonfiction texts on a related topic" when they are reading a novel with their students (Lemov 2010, 23).

> Recently, when reading Lily's Crossing, a novel set in World War II–era New York City, students stopped after a couple chapters to read an article on the rationing of supplies during that time. . . . They gained additional perspective on events in the novel with other such articles as they went through it.
>
> Now, the novel makes more sense because you understand about rationing, and the nonfiction article has meaning because you have come to care about Lily and [have] seen it through her experience. . . . (23)

Letting students experience a variety of texts and perspectives gives them a better sense of ownership of their reading lives.

This means that some of the details and interpretations we love best about some of our favorite works may not get the attention they would in a teacher-centered classroom. Allowing time for students to read and think about additional texts may also mean we don't read as many of our favorite works as we have in the past. However, the works we do read will be met with enthusiasm, engagement, and serious thought. They will also give students opportunities to practice the skills we want them to carry into adulthood: reading carefully, weighing perspectives, and thinking critically.

A more important concern is the impact nonfiction/informational text could have on teaching struggling readers and English language learners. While literary themes, conflict, characters, and plots have the potential to connect with these students, they may not see those connections without context. Because we love the literature we teach, we must not entertain the slightest notion that we cannot discover and create a learning pathway for English learners, as well as for students who may have less familiarity with a time period, theme, setting, or historical context. Incorporating nonfiction gives us the opportunity to give these students direct instruction in reading informational texts.

In "Cutting to the Common Core: Analyzing Informational Text," Kate Kinsella, educator and parent, describes the challenges informational texts can present:

> My own son, an English learner, is elated that his elementary English language arts coursework now includes a weekly news periodical, providing opportunities for him to learn about current events. For a recent homework assignment, however, he was flummoxed by the questions that required specifying the location of the evidence he obtained from the selection to support a claim . . .

Modeling the process of previewing an entire text to gauge text complexity then breaking it down into manageable segments for detailed reading and study is essential support for developing readers. Under-prepared students have rarely learned the cognitive secrets of siblings or high-achieving students who have successfully managed tomes of content-area reading. They rely on their teachers to demystify the process of reading to learn and guide them in developing a consistent, productive process for tackling challenging assignments. Without explicit, interactive in-class guidance, ill-equipped readers plow into a research article as if they were approaching a short story, starting on page one, with no sense of the text length, focus, structure, or more essential sections, and rarely make it beyond the introductory matter. (2014)

But struggling readers and English language learners are not the only students in our classrooms who need to learn how to read informational texts. As Duke and colleagues (2011) explain in *Reading and Writing Genre with Purpose*, "Readers and writers engage in different processes to different degrees when reading different kinds of texts. . . . Different genres have different features, [and] some effective approaches to reading and writing are tailored to specific genres" (6). If we want our students to become adults who are comfortable navigating any text they encounter, they need experience with a wide array of texts. As our study of literature helps them see themes, symbols, and the power of literary devices, the informational texts we use to support the literature help them identify and analyze opinions, weigh arguments, compare sources, and make decisions about what to believe.

ADDRESSING THESE CONCERNS

Having identified our concerns, we need to explore some practical ways to address them. They include:

- finding/selecting resources
- pairing/blending resources
- introducing nonfiction/informational texts
- monitoring and assessing students' progress.

Finding and Selecting Nonfiction/Informational Resources

We all know preparation time is in short supply. However, by leveraging the power of our professional learning community, everyone can work together to identify the learning objectives for nonfiction/informational texts and create a protean database of informational texts. This will not happen overnight: it has taken me years to collect the informational texts I now reference easily. However, the process has been as rewarding to me as the end result has been for my students. In my research, I dive into Twain's world, I listen to Poe's thinking, I consider Hawthorne's and Browning's writing, for example, with fresh eyes.

As you consider texts, keep in mind your students and their amazing questions. For example, when I introduced Emily Dickinson's poetry to my tenth graders years ago, even then, they were curious about the seeming lack of women's voices in literature. My eleventh graders were also curious about this apparent literary dearth. My seniors, too, expressed the same sentiments with regard to Brontë, Rossetti, and Browning—too few women—too much sublimation and punishment. So I looked for articles, essays, diaries, and poetry by late-nineteenth-century women I could blend with our study of Dickinson. The task in those pre-Internet days was daunting. However, the situation has changed over the years. Now when students ask me about the apparent dearth of women or about women characters they deem too quiet or too submissive or too indecisive, I have a wealth of both literary and nonfiction texts to cite and share with them.

We can also rely on our own knowledge of areas in which students could benefit from more background information. Whenever I read a piece of literature now, I think about what nonfiction might complement it. Conversely, when I read nonfiction/informational texts, I think about which pieces of literature students would understand and appreciate more if they had this information.

Figure 3.5

The Elevator, a nineteenth-century abolitionist newspaper

This is particularly true with regard to period literature, because many students today are unfamiliar with period vocabulary. When Jim, in Twain's *Adventures of Huckleberry Finn*, is explicating his definition of harem to Huck, he says: "A harem's a bo'd'n-house, I reck'n. Mos' likely dey has rackety times in de nussery. En I reck'n de wives quarrels considable; en dat 'crease de racket" (111). And while dialect poses its own extra effort, *harem* and *bo'd'n-house* can be impenetrable barriers to comprehension, especially thematic comprehension. Very few authors define or clarify vocabulary or social and historical contexts for their readers, and this affects the study of nineteenth-century American and British literature, Shakespeare, mythology, and other literary periods. To illustrate: in the lines above, Jim requires readers to access their knowledge of the Old Testament, King Solomon, ancient marriage structure, and a term that dates back to the 1700s. In the next, he blends the terms into his unique definition. Finally, he morphs this definition into an extended-explicit metaphor, revealing his bond to his family. I have found period articles from Garrison's *The Liberator* and Samuel Cornish's *The Elevator* useful in illustrating how biblical references were common in America at this time, and the advertisements of reputable boarding houses were on a par with advertisements of apartments and condos today, except for their unique and unbreakable restrictions (see Figure 3.5). Lively and energetic conversations take place among students and me about the culture, mores, and message Twain is conveying not only about these two characters but also about a time and a people.

Finally, poetry—yes, poetry—also offers nonfiction perspectives. The poems of Judith Ortíz Cofer are stellar examples, unique blendings of fiction and nonfiction/informational text. In an interview with Rafael Ocasio (2000), Ortíz Cofer says: "I cannot think of anything that I have done in fiction or nonfiction that has not found expression in either a successful or unsuccessful poem" (49). Although the Common Core State Standards may not view poetry as informational text, as teachers, we know that the autobiographical details we find in Cofer's "Quinceañera," for example, allow students to compare and contrast, explore, evaluate, and analyze poetry from earlier and contemporary periods to assess and measure the progressions and changes in perspective, voice, and sense of self. Our students' ability to see relevance in poetry extends as well to both canonical and modern poets: Tennyson, Chaucer, Brooks, Cullen, Bryant, Wordsworth, Rossetti, Whitman, Milton, Dove, Hughes, both Brownings, and Homer, for example.

As you select and blend nonfiction information texts, remember that a nonfiction/informational text should:

- complement the literary text
- provide insight, description, facts, background into the author, text, time period
- promote further exploration
- not be restricted to secondary research sources; what "texts" from the students' worlds could illuminate the literature?

Pairing/Blending Resources

Nonfiction/informational texts—especially primary sources—paired with literary texts can, as Aristotle suggests, grab the audience's imagination and curiosity. Consider:

- What aspect of the literary text does the nonfiction/informational text illustrate?
- Is there a similar theme, style, character, conflict, structure, point of view, setting?
- What is each author's purpose, audience, occasion?
- Are the texts different perspectives on the same topic?
- Do the texts take a similar but varied approach to the same topic?
- Does the informational text extend students' knowledge, helping them better understand the literary text?
- Does the informational text provide an opportunity for students to drill further into the literary text?

Introducing Nonfiction/Informational Texts

Once we're ready to use these resources in our classrooms, we turn our attention to our students, for whom we've done all this preparation: how will we introduce the texts to the class?

Independent Close Reading

At Woodberry Forest School, with an audience of boys, even highly motivated ones as these young men were, I had my work cut out for me. As I referenced earlier, their assigned reading was Douglass' *Narrative of the Life of Frederick Douglass*. I decided not to dive directly into the *Narrative* but rather to rely on primary, nonfiction/informational texts, hoping to peak the students' curiosity and interest. I also made sure that some of the documents were on my iPad (students today surround themselves with technology) and that they could hold other documents in their hands. Beginning this way allowed them to experience firsthand that the past is neither defunct nor irrelevant.

I chose four nonfiction/informational texts: "Why Should a Colored Man Enlist?" from *Douglass' Monthly*, April 1863; "To Our Patrons," *Freedom's Journal*, March 1827; The *Columbian Orator*, 1811, by Caleb Bingham; and the "Declaration of Sentiments" from the first women's rights conference, in Seneca Falls, New York, July 1848.

The students expected me to ask them about specific plot or style aspects of the texts. But I wanted to engage them from a different perspective. I began the Douglass classes, as discussed earlier, by asking two questions: What do you know about Douglass thus far? When do you think the first African American newspaper appeared? I passed around Douglass' article on my iPad. The students were surprised that I used my iPad, but more importantly, the article mesmerized them; I could see this reaction in their faces and in how long each student lingered, reading, on the page. As they passed the article along, the following questions emerged:

> Student 1: *Wow! So how did a slave get a newspaper?*
>
> Student 2: *What I want to know is who read his paper?*
>
> Student 3: *No, wait a minute; just how did he learn to write like this? I mean, we know his slave mistress taught him to read, but not like that—right?*

I was thrilled. They were doing what I wanted them to do—asking questions, drilling further into not only the texts but also into what caused them. I next showed them Bingham's *Columbian Orator* and explained, first, Douglass' attachment to it and, second, the rationale and place of rhetoric books in the nineteenth century. They were hooked. They began to thumb through Bingham's book, returning to certain sections, rereading sections, trying to align this new information with the *Narrative*. Each student made his own decisions about what other sections in the *Narrative*, the newspaper article, or the table of contents of *The Columbian Orator* to explore more closely to expand the class discussion from individual perspectives (see Figure 3.6). They lingered after each class to ask more questions.

They didn't read each text in its entirety, but segments of each sparked their curiosity, their critical thinking, their desire to read the Douglass autobiography. The iPad was new, but the rest of the approach was not. With my high school students in the past and with students today, I introduce nonfiction/informational text to trigger discoveries and conversations that lead us into the literary text in different and I hope relevant ways.

Collaborative Learning Communities

The cohort of educators with whom we work wanted to rethink the traditional grouping of students and, consequently, group work. Although some students work well independently, others prefer groups. But each of us remembered that this approach could be hit or miss and lacked overall coherence and consistency. We therefore developed a new approach to grouping—collaborative learning communities (CLCs). We would draw on our observations to form the CLCs during the first reporting period, and these communities would remain together for the academic year. Their members would converse, share, create projects, read and think, debate, and explore texts in class and beyond. Our goal was to place students in an environment conducive to their owning and assuming more responsibility for their work, with a teacher's guidance and monitoring. (When I work in a school for several days, I use an abbreviated version of this approach.)

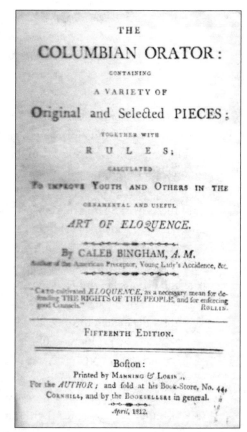

Figure 3.6
The Columbian Orator was an important resource for Douglass.

To determine whether the CLC objective could be achieved, we asked Kimberly N. Parker, a teacher at Cambridge Rindge and Latin School, in Massachusetts, to pilot our idea. Based on what she was teaching in her tenth-grade advanced placement English class, we created two thematic units. Each unit contained nonfiction/informational texts as complementary resources to the assigned literature. Thus far, Parker's and the students' comments have been insightful and instructive:

> Dr. Parker: *I wanted them to be able to synthesize multiple perspectives and evaluate arguments before ultimately coming to their own conclusions, something I'm certain they never would have been able to do without the supplemental texts I used to extend their understanding of the unit's objectives.*

Student: *Being presented with new ideas and themes about a text helps me further my own thinking and go deeper into topics that I hadn't thought much about. I can not only back up my own thoughts but also think about what the other ideas are and what they mean.*

Whole-Class Close Reading

This approach can be used singularly or in combination with one of the approaches discussed previously. I use it quite often with complex fiction and nonfiction to model the process, pose probing questions for critical thinking in lieu of providing summaries, and monitor student responses. Reading a piece of nonfiction/informational text with the whole class and then engaging students provides coherence and participation. I announce that I am not there to lecture. Rather, I am there to ask them questions, probe into the text, share and learn and explore together. They understand quickly that my intent is to engage each of them. A continuing result of this approach has been to interact with all students, not the few who always contribute. Although this approach takes patience and sometimes requires a few extra guided questions, it allows everyone to participate and express her or his insights.

With all of these suggested approaches, I encourage students to question, to disagree, to say, "I don't understand"; the objective is immersive engagement, critical thinking, and collaborative conversation and exploration of the assigned text.

These strategies are by no means exhaustive or encyclopedic, but they work—with all levels of students, regardless of ability, class, ethnicity, for example. My goal is never to posit what students cannot accomplish based on what they look like, where they come from, or the ability level to which they been assigned. I am most passionate about this stance, and it has stood me in good stead over the years, especially with high school students.

Tool 4:
Close Reading and Analysis Guide, Appendix B

Tool 5:
Close Reading Analysis Evaluation Rubric, Appendix C

Monitoring and Evaluating Students' Comprehension of Literary and Nonfiction/Informational Texts

With the methods suggested previously, I rely on a series of templates, but for informational reading alone, I rely on one rubric (see Appendix C) that assists and continues to inform me as I listen to class discussions and group-work conversations and review research projects. Students understand, can use, and even like this one. It allows them to control and own their learning. I also provide a fiction/nonfiction close reading and analysis guide (Appendix B) for students to use as they read texts independently, in groups, and as a class. (I don't describe the texts as *complex*, a currently popular term; I feel it can be off-putting.)

I realize these rubrics are extensive. They're meant to help you consider angles you might encourage students to explore in the works you are studying. Focusing on a few skills at a time and building on them as the year progresses may yield more understanding than trying to address the entire lengthy rubric with a single group of texts. You can also share applicable sections with students so they can track their own progress.

Knowing in which areas students are making advances and in which they require further help is the information you need to plan effective instruction. Ultimately, you want students to think about what they read, wrestle with it, and use the resulting knowledge and insight in their everyday life. Nonfiction/informational texts do not take away from students' experiences with literature or the significant impact literary works carry. Blending fiction and nonfiction/informational texts in ELA classes, K–12, enables students to take what they have read, heard, explored, and learned and apply it beyond the classroom.

We've devoted an entire chapter to discussing how informational text can inform the study of literature, but we would also like to take a moment to restate literature's importance on its own. As this wonderful anecdote from Mark Twain shows us, literature can reach readers in ways that nonfiction cannot.

At the dinner of the Nineteenth Century Club, Sam Clemens recalled a conversation he and Charles William Eliot, president of Harvard College, had a few years before about a meeting Eliot had with Charles Darwin. Eliot told Clemens,

"Do you know that there is one room in Darwin's house, his bedroom, where the housemaid is never allowed to touch two things? One is a plant he is growing and studying while it grows, and the other some books that lie on the night table at the head of his bed. They are your books, Mr. Clemens, and Mr. Darwin reads them every night to lull him to sleep." Clemens then told the group, "My friends, I thoroughly appreciated that compliment, and considered it the highest one that was ever paid to me. To be the means of soothing to sleep a brain teeming with bugs and squirming things like Darwin's was something that I had never hoped for." (November 20, 1900)

Making Literature Relevant

4

We are finally moving to a point where we can state the values of a literary education more clearly and forcefully, in terms that will justify just as much attention to literary study as our nation periodically invests in math, science, and "basic" literacy skills.
—Arthur N. Applebee, *Literature in the Secondary Schools: Studies of Curriculum and Instruction in the United States*

■

What gets left out of literacy, too often, is literature.
—Louann Reid, Colorado State University (personal communication, July 27, 2014)

THOSE OF US WHO LOVE LITERATURE may wonder why anyone would set aside Brontë's *Wuthering Heights* or Anaya's *Bless Me, Ultima* and, instead, read seventy pages (or a myriad of websites) full of numbing prose that summarizes the plots in a disjointed way, without any hint of voice or even humanity. Yet, secondary English students do this regularly. As student-reporter Laila Abtahi (2010) explains in "Should Students Study with Sparknotes? Con" for *The Mirador Online*, the Orinda, California, Miramonte High School newspaper, "SparkNotes temporarily assures a student that his or her grade is safe." In contrast, student-reporter, Caroline Cook (2010), in "Should Students Study with Spark Notes? Pro" asserts that SparkNotes are equal to the best secondary sources in "guiding" students and teachers through the mire of "confusing schoolwork . . . SparkNotes is an effective secondary source because it provides supplemental study guides, and helps students understand these assignments." Students not only choose to read summaries instead of literature, they also trust those summaries to be guides and mentors.

Have we somehow unwittingly contributed to this trend? If our students are not embracing literature, perhaps we have not transmitted to them our innate passion for literature. Perhaps instead of trusting this love to be transmitted through some form of natural absorption, we might consciously construct collaborative, discoverable teaching moments that will pique students' interest and curiosity, prompting them to read instead of relying on—and trusting—shortcuts. As we reassert our voices and reaffirm our passion for literature, we must also listen to and observe how our students relate to and interact with the literature we teach:

- How do we engage a literary text not for ourselves but for our students?
- How can we enable students to engage that same literary text?

If we can make literature relevant not only for us, but for our twenty-first-century students, they will read, will not disconnect what they read in our classes from what they read outside, and will not view reading literature as a chore.

In 1987, seven organizations, including the National Council of Teachers of English (NCTE) and the Modern Language Association (MLA), created and convened a coalition of sixty educators to discuss, explore, and examine common issues and concerns in the teaching of English language arts—including the issue of students' not reading. Their guiding questions, centered on the students' perspective on learning and engagement and their perception of the relevance of literature, underscore the attention given to student engagement and identify concerns we still face today:

- What are the conditions under which literature is being taught?
- What are the traditions represented in the selections for study?
- What are teachers' goals for student learning?
- How do these goals work themselves out in classroom practice?

Arthur Applebee's *Literature in the Secondary Schools: Studies of Curriculum and Instruction in the United States* (1993) is based on the resulting studies.

HOW DO WE ENGAGE A LITERARY TEXT?

We approach a piece of literature as a bifurcated audience: English majors and teachers. As English majors, we joyfully enter a piece of literature with an attitude of discovery, curiosity, exploration, diversity, and wonderment. We lose ourselves in the words, characters, scenes, conflicts; the stylistic nuances thrill us. One visual I love when attending NCTE's annual convention is the tremendous suitcases filled with the books teachers are eagerly bringing home—so many that few even try to lift them. On every face are the most wonderful, satisfying smiles, for each suitcase contains amazing adventures, overwhelming tragedies, seeming and actual insurmountable challenges, real people just like us, and bigger-than-life people who keep us in absolute awe. We cheer protagonists and loathe antagonists. Gordian knot–like plots—Laurence Sterne's *Tristram Shandy*, Toni Morrison's *Beloved*, Shakespeare's *The Tragedy of King Lear*, William Faulkner's "A Rose for Emily" or *The Sound and Fury*, William Blake's *The Marriage of Heaven and Hell*, Dante's *La Divina Commedia*, and Isabel Allende's *House of the Spirits*—keep us welded to our seats, whether in a room, on a subway, under a tree, on a beach.

As English language arts teachers, our first wish is for our students to love literature as much as we do. Graduate students with a passion to teach English always have the same response when I ask, "Why do you want to teach English?" Without exception, it's "Because I love to read, and I want to help students love to read, too." My follow-up question, "What do you want for your students after they leave your class and graduate; what do you want them to GET?" is something of a conundrum, but most agree they want their students to love literature. This is a serious sort of "no response," because it precludes not only the literal purpose of English language arts but also its import and place on our students' lives. The response I want to hear focuses on how English language arts prepares students, speaks to our and our students' here and now—their realities both in and outside class. We know the power of literature and the ways in which it can touch the lives of those who love it, and sharing that love is powerful. However, we must also consider that each of us is one of only a handful of teachers who will try to help a particular student hone the literacy skills he or she will need as an adult. Ernest Morrell and colleagues (2013) remind us that what we teach lives and functions long after students have graduated and that we "have to think differently about how we teach, the tools we use, and the products that we demand from our students" (19).

Also meriting reflection and concern is our desire for students to understand the texts as we understand them. We have all had students who make an abrupt right (or left) turn when we and the other students continue straight ahead without considering or even being curious about an alternative path. More often these students aren't deliberate contrarians, but engage with the material differently and have a divergent point of view. Sometimes, we dismiss their comments because they did not address the assignment as we have envisioned it. But students may not always resonate with or comprehend a character, event, or theme as we or literary critics have interpreted it. (See Figures 4.1 and 4.2.)

Taylor
Mr. Mulreany
AP Language and Composition
14 January

The Effects and Defects of Parental Figures in *Huck Finn*

Typically families provide a sense of structure and belonging to the various members included. Parental figures within those family units help stimulate the feeling of acceptance by taking on the roles of caretaker, educator, and protector. Whichever way these roles are upheld or neglected by the parents or guardians shapes the child's mentality and behaviors. Families, biological or symbolic, are recurring themes in Mark Twain's *Adventures of Huckleberry Finn*. In Twain's novel, the connections between the parental figure and the child mimics family-type relationships: the Widow and Huck, Pap and Huck, and Jim and Huck. even though these couples may not all be connected biologically, their time together creates unique ties. These connections define and drive Huck's lifestyle choices, ultimately constructing the *Adventures of Huckleberry Finn*.

Figure 4.1
Taylor's paper, "The Effects and Defects of Parental Figures in *Huck Finn*" takes a fresh perspective on Twain's work, making an eye-opening comparison between the families depicted in *Huck Finn* and modern-day understandings of family.

Micayla
Ms. Christopherson
AP Lang and Comp
25 Jan

Twain's Childhood Influence on *The Adventures of Huckleberry Finn*

Science explains that memories are just neurons firing synapses back and forth across the brain as chemicals that allow images and events to be permanently recorded in the mind. Science does not explain how these singular events combined provide a foundation for thought and individual personality that transposes time and later has a significant influence on future situations. Memories from childhood are but one of the events that affect later decisions. The novel, *The Adventures of Huckleberry Finn,* written by Mark Twain, was greatly influenced by the childhood experiences he had in his hometown Hannibal, Missouri. The events and people in Twains life inspired the relationships between Huckleberry Finn and the following characters: Jim, Tom, his family, and the Mississippi River.

The novel is a chronological timeline that describes the circumstances that the main character, Huckleberry Finn, endured when he sailed down the Mississippi River with a runaway slave. The entire novel is set in Hannibal, Missouri, and along the Mississippi River. The childhood persona of Mark Twain shaped the tone of the book. Small details, such as when Huck is jealous or disappointed, aid the reader in developing a personal relationship with Huck, and allow themselves to relate on a basic human understanding. Huck also is subject to physical needs. He requires water, shelter, food, and once says, "I didn't want to go to sleep, of course; but I was so sleepy I couldn't help it; so I thought I would take just one little cat-nap" (Twain). His essential and unwilling need to sleep adds vulnerability to Huck's character, which creates a kinship with the readers, and Twain himself. His childhood was not easy, because he was forced to work, and all a child needs at times is to have the ability to become vulnerable and submit to the most basic instincts.

The relationship that Mark Twain developed between Huck Finn and the slave Jim was a reflection of the friendship Twain had with slaves as a child. Jim was the slave on the farm where Huck was given shelter and learned how to read. He had always been a prevalent presence because he was large in stature and performed most of the work. Huck treated him rudely in the beginning of the novel, reflecting how society saw the slaves. As the plot develops, and more time is spent between the two, Huck's personal feelings and ideas shift. This occurrence is especially prevalent when Huck, motivated by personal guilt and morals, apologizes to Jim, ". . . before I could work myself up to go and humble myself to a nigger; but I done it, and I warn't ever sorry for it afterwards, neither" (Twain). Huck displays his realization that blacks have humanity, and all humans deserve a fair treatment and respect, as apologizing is one of the most significant ways to demonstrate respect, because it shows humility and a genuine concern

(continues)

Figure 4.2
Micayla's paper uses Twain's own childhood and upbringing and that of slaves he observed as a child—images of family, familiar and different—as lenses in her analysis of *Adventures of Huckleberry Finn.*

for the opposing party's feelings. Twain is attempting to weave and thread basic morals in scenes such as this one, because it adds to the development and characterization of each individual. Twain personally relates to this moral journey, because it was inspired by his own childhood of attempting to learn the morals that were acceptable in society. The act of apologizing is also significant due to Huck's age, and for him to have the initiative and integrity to apologize without any prompting reflects how his character has matured as the friendship between himself and the slave. The friendship with Jim also showed Huckleberry Finn where the line in society lies. He could be friends with Jim, but not all would approve of the choice. Negroes still were considered property at this point in history. Huck would have to accept that legally he was above Jim on the social standing, and not let that affect his personal opinion of him. This parallels what Twain learned early in his childhood, when he stated: "All the negroes were friends of ours, and with those of our own age we were in effect comrades, and yet not comrades; color and condition interposed a subtle line which both parties were conscious of, and which rendered complete fusion impossible" (Smith). The innocence of children has allowed the boundary to be pushed enough to develop true friendship. Twain demonstrates this in his own childhood friendship with a black boy. He believed that they are not mere animals, with no thoughts or feelings, but people who could experience emotions and have opinions, and expressed this belief by emphasizing the symbolic relationship between Huckleberry Finn and Jim the slave.

Figure 4.2 (*continued*)

In December 2014 while a group of students and I were discussing some of Mark Twain's books, one student, Taylor (referenced in Figure 4.1), wondered whether Twain was aware he was foreshadowing things to come with regard to parenting and family paradigms. From this Generation Z student's perspective, which was well thought out, Twain had tapped into familial constructs not common until the late twentieth and early twenty-first century: blended families; single-parent families; extended families; abusive, caring, ambivalent, broken families. Amazing, absolutely amazing. In many years of reading and teaching Twain, I had never thought of this critical interpretation from such a perspective, nor of exploring such a potentially sensitive issue with high school students, nor had I or anyone I knew pursued this line of investigation. Other students found equally fascinating questions in the work, such as, "How inspired was Twain by the women in his life? Was the feminism, or sometimes the apparent lack of it, in the story representative of what Twain experienced in his life, with the women he surrounded himself with?" and "Are there any repeating language (literary and rhetorical) devices that you have noticed Twain used to characterize women and the events that pertain to them?"

Unless students feel comfortable and safe, exploring and stretching their intellect and curiosity, we will miss out on new perspectives and ideas about a well known and loved text. Judith Langer (2000) describes the issue this way:

Applebee (1984) found that students are often asked simply to display their knowledge rather than to explain, defend, or elaborate on what they are learning. Langer and Applebee (1987) and Langer (1992) report that teachers tend to focus on particular content to be learned to the neglect of ways in which their students think about that content. (3)

Applebee describes this instructional tendency as "the teacher-centered classroom," in which students are not encouraged—intentionally or unintentionally—to explore and develop their own unique ideas and thoughts when reading literature (201). I describe this situation, much like Freire does, as one in which students are on a static, "listening-object," pathway of either right or wrong answers resulting in a dearth of cumulative learning (Chadwick 2015):

This kind of delivery in teaching does not foment creativity, curiosity, much less, dialectical conversation among students or between teacher and students, unless, of course, students themselves have these conversations outside of class—as some of us did. Even conferences to "discuss" essays are some-times one-way rather than an exploration and guided mentoring leading to a "learning for under-standing" moment. (101)

One clear example of the opposite of this approach occurred in the fourth-grade class of which I was a member:

My music appreciation teacher was amazing, and we all excitedly looked forward to her coming to us twice weekly. Although I cannot remember her name, what I do remember and what yet affects my life today was her love and passion for classical music and her ability to translate it for us to foment our own appreciation and, for some, a love, for it.

As a teacher myself now, I can look back and see that her delivery was protean: each visit had clear, targeted objectives for the fourth-grade audience; each session included a focus on an instru-ment—we could see it, touch it, hear it; each session included a piece of classical music featuring the instrument; each session included her talking about the "story, or narrative," of the piece and the com-poser; each session always included her asking us what we thought, what we heard, what we felt about what we heard. Complementing the selections, she included opera—quite conducive, actually, because of the attending characters, plots, conflicts, for example. To make all she did in class have immediate relevance, she took us on field trips to Jones Hall in Houston to see, listen, and experience opera in real time. My first was Madame Butterfly. *As an ongoing added follow-up, she required us to watch Leonard Bernstein's Young People's Concerts with the New York Philharmonic on Saturdays or Sundays. Like her, Bernstein targeted his performance by talking to the audience for younger listeners.*

This example illustrates a fundamental and dynamic relationship between students and teacher—not static, not passive. We were not mere receptacles nor she and Bernstein the ultimate deliverers.

These learning moments, which had their origin in a fourth-grade classroom, extended through grade 6 and into our lives outside of the school itself, and I dare say, for some of us, beyond our communities, our states, and country. Relying on this kind of instruction, our teacher, and Bernstein, too, allowed us to transcend time and space and culture into many learning moments. Dewey describes this kind of learning as learning that occurs in and out of class. (Chadwick 2015, 102)

What I find wonderful about collaborating with teachers around the country now is their growing curiosity about and eager embrace of new learning pathways. One has only to attend local and national meetings of educators, be part of a Professional Learning Community, or read conversations and collaborations taking place in organizations' and connected communities' blogs and Twitter exchanges to witness this willingness to practice and create active learning experiences.

<table>
<tr><td>

Tool 6:

Rereading Template,

Appendix D

</td><td>

Rereading Literature to Help Us See Our Students' Needs

</td></tr>
</table>

To make literature relevant to our students, we must consider their viewpoints as well as our own. Of course, we all undoubtedly do this to one degree or another each day, considering the details of a text from our students' perspectives can yield valuable insights. As Paulo Freire (1998, 2005) writes:

[T]hose who teach learn, on the one hand, because they recognize previously learned knowledge and, on the other, because by observing how the novice student's curiosity works to apprehend what is taught (without which one cannot learn), they help themselves to uncover uncertainties, rights, and wrongs. . . . [Teachers'] learning in their teaching is observed to the extent that, humble and open, teachers find themselves continually ready to rethink what has been thought and to revise their positions. Their learning lies in their seeking to become involved in their students' curiosity and in the paths and streams it takes them through. (51–52)

The Rereading Template (Appendix D) lets us see our reading styles and predilections on three levels—as an avid reader/English major, as a teacher, and from the perspective of our students. I apply this strategy each time I work with high school students.

The rubric includes questions about preferences as well as the construction of the text—total length, plot complexity, and so on. When we consider relevance to students, we must also consider how well the students can access the text. If they are likely to be daunted by a long book or ornate language, we need to consider how we can help them meet these demands.

I recommend using this template before you begin to teach a particular work so you can use your findings as you plan your unit. If you find yourself wondering how a particular student might react to a given element, listen even more closely to that student in the days or weeks leading up to the unit so as to better understand his or her point of view.

Rereading a text from another's perspective has also been valuable for my graduate students, who have learned to combat censorship by first scrutinizing the challenged texts from the perspectives of teachers, students, and parents. I'll admit to some grumbling about this painstaking approach when I assigned it, but I still hear from and collaborate with some of the students, and when they tell me how they have incorporated our rereading method into their own teaching, I know we did the right thing.

When teachers and I discuss Frost's "The Road Not Taken," for example, we first distinguish between our innate love for the poem and its potential meaning and complexity for our students. Unlike writers whom students initially perceive as impenetrable, such as Shakespeare, T. S. Eliot, Nikki Giovanni, Pound, and Whitman, they often see a poet like Frost as easier to explore. However, as we know, what appears easy is often subtly complex, requiring even closer attention. Such is the case with most of Frost's poems (and prose texts by Hemingway, Fitzgerald, and Hurston, for that matter).

As we literally slow down and reread the Frost piece from several points of view, we see that the narrator has chosen a path that appears less traveled but in reality is just as worn as the other. But having chosen the "less" traveled one has made a difference for the narrator. What that difference is—positive or negative—she or he does not reveal. This allows us to teach inference; subliminal messages based on cultural archetypes and mind-sets; symbolic images (a wood, two paths, the journey metaphor); and the poet's style and use of language. It also allows us to privilege and hear our students' voices and ideas and queries.

Reflecting on my teaching approaches, my goals for my students, and the conditions under which students experience the literature (Applebee 1993, 201), I realized that I needed to hone my listening skills; "park" my English-major relationship with the text; privilege students' voices, questions, and perspectives; and say to students, especially high school students, "I do not have all the answers. If you ask a question, and I don't know, I will tell you I don't know. But, I promise we will find it together." Ernest Morrell (2008) further reiterates this needed and focused learning pathway with our twenty-first-century students as audience:

> As a secondary English teacher, I was initially appalled by the disconnect that existed between the students' out of school literacies and the world of the literacy classroom. . . . I merely had a strong belief

> *I know how to write forever. . . . It's mine. It's free. . . . It's pure knowledge. . . . Let the reader enter with her or his own imagination, and that makes us co-conspirators, as it were, together—the reader and me.*
>
> —Toni Morrison (2015)

that students possessed brilliance and passion that were being neither acknowledged nor accessed inside of literacy classrooms.... I had to find a way to achieve success with my English students or something inside of me was going to die....

Although I never lost sight of the importance of academic literacy development, I became increasing interested in the connections between a critical pedagogy of popular culture and the development of critical literacies. (91–93)

HOW DO WE ENABLE STUDENTS TO ENGAGE THAT SAME LITERARY TEXT?

We are teaching students the literary texts we read and love. The difference lies in the purpose for reading and—something not often considered—choice. We choose to read these texts; our students most often are told what they will read. How do we encourage and enable students' wanting to read—how do we tickle their curiosity? I have seen the following strategies work time and again:

- Present the text not only as an assignment but as an adventure. Assure students that as they read the book, they will learn not only about the characters, their fictional world, and the obstacles they encounter, but also about themselves and how these same challenges are often an important part of their world.
- Discuss with students the types of books they read on their own outside class. What interests them about their selected books and what have they learned from reading them?
- Review the setting and background of the assigned text. Supply images and documents, even sounds, especially when students are unfamiliar with a location or event or time. When and where does the story take place? Why is this important? How would students live if they were in the same setting and what would their lives be like?
- What challenges are students likely to encounter while reading the book—difficulties with names, customs, cultural issues, provocative situations, profanity, violence, lifestyle issues? Help students understand the relevance of these issues and why they are included. Address their possible discomfort with the issues and the possibility of their initial rejection of the novel because of them.
- Introduce the characters. Who are they? Where is the novel set (time, location)? What is going on in the characters' lives and in the world around them?
- Encourage students to cite specific moments in the text that trouble them and explain what they do not like about the author's decision to include such language, situations, and actions.
- Discuss how literature is sometimes "messy," why that is important, and how the book fits into the general purpose and goals of literature even if reading it is sometimes uncomfortable.

These strategies help me every time I walk into a classroom. They have changed over time and will continue to do so, but the essential goals remain the same. I find it fascinating how closely this process parallels what Toni Morrison recommended in her responses to queries my Twain, Faulkner, and Morrison course students, all future educators, posed in writing. The questions my students asked focused on memory and sensitive topics, often found in literature—how teachers prepare both text and instruction and how teachers might approach students so that their curiosity, their own sense of relevance, and their predilection towards argumentation and analysis would emerge. My students were echoing concerns that challenge many ELA teachers across the country. Morrison advised them to "put the subject [of racism] on an intellectual plane first, to avoid as much subjectivity as possible in a topic that is rife with emotion." Rather than focusing on blame, she suggests analysis—of the facts of specific situations and of the language used to frame actions and motives.

A crucial issue with my graduate students has been developing their rapport and collaboration with their students. Reflecting, listening, journaling, collaborating—these are our guideposts for instigating engaging and immersive experiences. I encourage them to share concerns, ideas, issues—anything they want to question or explore. I encourage them to be proactive in their instructional approaches and to be advocates for their students even if it means taking a risk.

Logan Manning (2001) approached me about this issue: "Professor Chadwick, my students won't read anything. I don't quite know what I need to do to encourage them to read. Any suggestions?" What made her dilemma not only fascinating but also prescient was her desire and decision to entertain different learning pathways and approaches. What happened follows, with brief but pointed explications of the actual instructional process practiced in both my Methods of Teaching English and Twain, Faulkner, Morrison courses. She remembers the situation this way:

In my first year teaching, I taught students who were repeating the ninth grade. Most of them had been involved in the juvenile justice system. Most of them had never imagined themselves or been validated as successful students. Most of them had never had the experience of loving a book. Carrying the stigma of school failure, these youth were not generally invited to imagine with unfettered possibilities. Having struggled to engage these students whose persistently negative histories with school created justifiable barriers to classroom learning, I learned with them the power of narrative to help students imagine different endings to their own stories. That first year it was our reading of Always Running (Rodriguez 1993), the memoir of a former gang member that helped students embrace possibilities for change in their own lives.

The students in my classroom that year came to school despite tremendous challenges. Because of the bussing system in the city of Boston, many of them took several trains and busses to get to school. Yet when these youths arrived in the schoolhouse, many were labeled students who "did not want to *learn" by teachers who struggled to engage them in classroom learning. I too struggled to engage them and to justify how our learning in ELA would serve them in their lives. This seemed an especially difficult task when using unwieldy literature textbooks that weren't exactly inviting.*

So began our challenge. My mind flashed back to my own first years of teaching and my remedial students—mostly of color, mostly poor, mostly invisible. Logan earnestly believed in literacy for all students, and her determination and passion to help these students was clear to me—and close to me. Our first concern was to understand Logan's audience and to acknowledge they had never read a book before. I recommended that she not simply assign a text but give them a proposition for reading—to put some control into their hands by empowering their voices. Again, Logan remembers:

After surveying the youths and discovering that the overwhelming majority of them claimed they disliked reading or hadn't read anything that they enjoyed, I felt my job that year had to be to engage them in a reading experience that they would enjoy and find relevant to their lives. Many of the students in the program had experiences with gangs and gang violence either because of personal association or because of the neighborhoods where they lived. Students commonly wore RIP hoodies commemorating young people who had died as a result of urban violence. The issue was present in the hallways and in class, but it was not being addressed through the curriculum. I decided to teach Always Running: La Vida Loca: Gang Days in L.A. *that spring because it was of high interest and would nurture a space for talking about some of the critical issues the students faced outside of school. My graduate school professor knew the author, Luis Rodriguez, and she reached out to him to see if he would talk with the class. We created an incentive: if the class could read the book and complete the assignments, they would be rewarded with a field trip to Harvard University and a conference call with Luis Rodriguez.*

Enabling students to engage the same literary text demands that we find identification pathways to relevance even if we initially feel there are no points for identification. At this juncture, I acknowledge Kenneth Burke (1969), who long ago understood this seemingly disparate juxtaposition:

To begin with "identification" is, by the same token, though roundabout, to confront the implications of division. . . . Identification is affirmed with earnestness precisely because there is division. Identification is compensatory to division. If men were not apart from one another, there would be no need for the rhetorician to proclaim their unity. If men were wholly and truly of one substance, absolute communication would be of man's very essence. It would not be an ideal, as it now is, partly embodied in material conditions and partly frustrated by these same conditions; rather, it would be as natural, spontaneous, and total as with those ideal proto-types of communication, the theologian's angels, or "messengers." (22)

The difference in and concomitant necessity for identification creates relevance for our students. From this perspective, no piece of literature—not one by Shakespeare, Baldwin, Alexie, Brontë, Tolstoy, Tennyson, Lorde, or even Henry James—can be unassailable.

We chose Luis Rodriguez's *Always Running: La Vida Loca: Gang Days in L.A.* for these students because we believed his personal narrative, beautifully and viscerally written, with vivid metaphors and similes about young people, challenges, peer pressure, fears, and aspirations, would achieve identification and, ultimately, relevance.

For their first book, Logan's students required relevance—not because they were mostly of color, not because they were mostly poor, but because they felt invisible and lacked voice and identity. Like the women featured in Belzer's "'I Don't Crave to Read'" (2002), they had never connected with assigned texts. Time and time again in studies and reports and in classrooms, students state lack of relevance, lack of clear connection, as a deterrent to their reading (111–12). To provide incentive and motivation for the students, I contacted Rodriguez to ask whether he would help.

Logan delivered the proposition to her students: "Would you consider reading Luis

I believe that a "literacy bridge," however one defines it, must be built from both banks and meet somewhere near the middle. This is a way of saying that any communication—typographic, online, aural—fails if it involves nothing more than a sender transporting "content" to a recipient. I have tried to make my narratives collaborative, by writing in a way that invites the reader to come along with me on a journey of alert discovery. I want the reader to "see" the people and their movements, and the physical places they inhabit, that I have tried to capture in words. I want the reader to "hear" the human voices as they speak in their distinctive cadences and vernacular, and to hear the truths and deceptions, conscious and unconscious, that the speech reveals. I want the reader to "smell" the damp leaves on the curving road that made the car skid and the fresh blood afterward. I want my work to offer the essential raw materials that will awaken the reader's active critical and moral consciousness regarding the heart of the story—even if, and perhaps especially if the reader's view departs from my own. If all goes well, we will meet, at story's end, atop the finished bridge's girders, protected, by words and thought that we've built, from falling.

—Ron Powers, author and Pulitzer Prize–winning journalist (November 29, 2014)

Rodriguez's *Always Running: La Vida Loca: Gang Days in L.A.* if you would have an opportunity to speak with Mr. Rodriguez and ask him questions? But you would have to agree to read the book." Knowing that literacy, education, and urban children of color were key issues of his writing and social outreach, I called Rodriguez, explained the situation, and asked whether he would help. I told him I would ask my department chair at Harvard whether we could have a date and time for the high school students to take a field trip and share a conference call with him. Logan remembers:

> When I first proposed the idea to the class, there were many eyes rolling. Students were not going to be sold on the idea so easily and they insisted that they wouldn't make it through a whole book. They were amused at the idea of traveling to Harvard because, while it was just a train ride away, it may as well have been in another universe. Because these students had all experienced school failure, they did not imagine themselves in that space.

But she did persuade her students:

> Not taking no for an answer, I placed Always Running at the center of our work as a class. In the beginning we read aloud and I invited students to discuss the book together.

Logan experienced other, unexpected hurdles: no books, no budget to purchase them, and reticence by the school administration to sanction a field trip. These were overcome. Thanks to a donor, Logan was able to give each of her students a copy of the book that was theirs to keep (most of them had never had a book of their own). The school did sanction the field trip. We scheduled a visit to the Harvard Graduate School of Education, where the class would use a conference room to have a group call with the Rodriguez.

The students did read the book, and they used a revised version of my Students' Literary Analysis Rubric (Appendix E) as they dove deeply and wholeheartedly into the text.
Logan remembers:

> In the beginning we read aloud, and I invited students to discuss the book together. Slowly they became engaged in the story, and they identified with the imagery and the dilemmas described by the author. They began to ask questions and make connections to their lived experiences. They wrote in journals and they reflected on what they were taking away from the narrative. They got hooked. The students who insisted they would not make it through the book found themselves flipping through the pages and wanting to know what would happen next. We finished the book together, and many of the students said it was the first time they had enjoyed reading something. They were eager to celebrate their accomplishment with my professor and the author.

Reading Deeply

Langer (2000) asserts that as students read, their envision-ments ("what the reader understands, the questions that develop, and the hunches that arise about how the piece might unfold" [7]) change:

The envisionments change as the reading progresses because as reading continues, some information is no longer important, some is added, and some is reinterpreted. What readers come away with at the end of a reading includes what they understand, what they don't, and the questions and hunches they still have. (7–8)

As students connect with a text, they are not only more willing to examine it closely, they are eager to do so. The Students' Literary Analysis Rubric (Appendix E) is "something in hand" to guide and facilitate independent and collaborative reading, discussion, and analysis.

As Burke (1969) and Langer (2000, 8–11) explain, students' processing of reading emerges in stages: literal reading, relational reading, consubstantiality/identification, and comprehension. Literal reading involves the basics: character(s), plot, setting, conflict; it's important but only the first step, not be an end in itself. Relational reading, as Langer describes, is "being inside and moving through" a text; readers begin comparing and contrasting our own experiences to characters or events in the text. Langer continues, "This is the time when meaning begets meaning; we are caught up in the narrative of a story, the sense or feel of a poem the imagery of description, or the mellifluousness of a beautiful oratory" (18). Consubstantiality/identification, for Burke, represents a critical aim of a writer, seeking the reader's identification with the acts and actors in the text, thereby developing a relationship:

A doctrine of consubstantiality, either explicit or implicit, may be necessary to any way of life. For substance, in the old philosophies, was an act; and a way of life is an acting-together; and in acting together, men have common sensations, concepts, images, ideas, attitudes that make them consubstantial. (Burke 1969, 21)

Finally, with comprehension, readers experience and understand the text to the extent we can use it to make meaning for ourselves beyond the text, "when we have the knowledge or insight available to use in new and sometimes unrelated situations. It is generative in that we apply critical aspects of one richly developed envisionment toward the creation of a new envisionment-building experience" (Langer 2000, 21). An illustration of this concept is presented in Chapter 5,

"Blending the Canon with the New," using Thoreau's "Civil Disobedience" in connection with an event occurring in New England during 2014 that was reported nationally. Overall, ELA teachers hope that reading literature will result in students' using the literature in life and career.

The Students' Literary Analysis Rubric (Appendix E) reflects these types of reading, as well as my and others' research and observations. All the templates and rubrics in this book are organic and intentionally mobile. Students profoundly impact my revisions and adjustments because they are never the same from class to class, region to region, and especially year to year. And because students today are highly mobile and socially networked, I design rubrics and charts students can use inside and outside class, independently and collaboratively. They can use hard copies or digital versions. They can respond in the spaces provided or in a notebook or digital journal. Most importantly, this tool belongs to the students: it is not an assignment to be returned and graded for correctness and completeness. It is a framework to challenge students' thinking, to give shape to their thoughts, and to push them toward critical thought.

Going Where They'd Never Gone Before: The Harvard Field Trip

Logan's students had read the book. The day for the field trip and conference call arrived. The adult educators accompanying Logan and her students knew they were not allowed to contribute or intervene while the students were talking with Rodriguez; this conversation was theirs alone. Logan and I were excited and eager and anticipatory, trying to prepare for everything, anything. The students walked gingerly and quietly onto Appian Way where the School of Education is located and into Longfellow Hall. Their reticence did not surprise me. I remembered my experiences with my students during the first few days in my remedial English classes: they sized me up and felt out of place, particularly when I explained that we really were going to "have school," as they termed it.

Logan's students walked into a very quiet conference room containing a large circular table, a conference phone in the center, surrounded by comfortable chairs. Logan introduced me to each of her students; each uttered a barely audible but polite hello. I thanked the students for coming and reiterated to the adults that they were welcome but could not participate in the conference call. I called Rodriguez, and the wonderment of the day began—not so quiet, not so traditional, and definitely not so expected. I introduced Rodriguez and asked students to provide their names when they spoke to him. Then I listened and observed and learned.

Student 1: *So, did you really write this book? I mean, is it really about you?*

Rodriguez: *Yes, I wrote the book and the book is about my life and me. But this book is also about the lives of my friends, so many who are now dead. This book is also about my son.*

Student 2: *Why did you want to write about gangs?*

Rodriguez: *I write about my life. My life was in L.A. with gangs. I lived the gang life and thought it was what I wanted. You guys tell me, why did you read the whole book?*

Various Students: *Because we were told to. Yeah, we were told to, but then we liked it. Yeah, it was reading, but not like reading you know? Yeah, not boring.*

I'd promised Rodriguez we would not take more than an hour of his time, but the session lasted two hours. The students referenced pages and scenes in the narrative, and Rodriguez asked them about specific moments in the text. They drilled into choices he made, challenges he confronted. As the students felt more at ease not only with the environment but also with Rodriguez, the adults melted away; *we* became invisible. The students were alone in this safe room with this writer whose book they had just read. I learned much that day about engagement, identification, and relevance and the power literature has for our students. Of the many exchanges I recorded in my journal, this one remains ever with me, especially when I am with high school students:

Student 3 (a young lady): *I want to ask you a question, but I'm not sure how to say it, exactly.*

Rodriguez: *Just say it; you are safe here and can say anything to me you want.*

Student 3: *I'm in a gang. I don't want to die. How do I stay out of the grave like you did?*

Rodriguez: *You don't have to die. Get out of the gang and stay in school. But this takes courage, and I know each of you in this room has that courage from listening to you today. Your homies may not want you to leave them, but you have to, to survive. The streets have nothing; remember that. Stay in school. Learn. You know what I'm saying?*

You could have heard the proverbial pin drop. Never before had I witnessed students so intensely connected into a piece of literature. When offered the learning opportunity, these students accepted the challenge, read a book for the first time, left their school and traveled to a university, talked to and listened to the author of the book.

The students began that afternoon quiet and reticent. They left the room animated, talking about parts of the book they now wanted to reread, talking about their impression of Luis Rodriguez. They also talked about themselves, no longer invisible. They held on to their books, books they now owned. I was convinced they had read every word—the covers of these once new books now showed wear—and they had shown us all the power of literature under the guidance of a passionate and determined teacher, Logan Manning. I have quoted to students more often than I can remember Aristotle's conviction in *The Poetics* that great literature moves people to act. I have always believed this to be true. On that day, with those students, Logan, and Rodriguez, I absolutely knew it to be true. (See Figure 4.3 for thank-you notes that students wrote to Luis Rodriguez.)

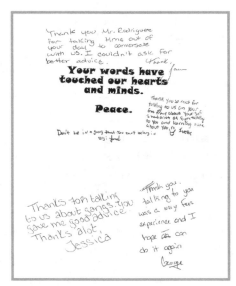

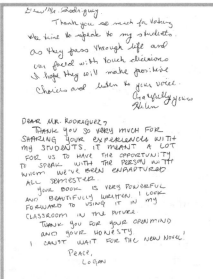

Figure 4.3

Logan's students' notes of thanks to Luis Rodriguez

Logan's work with her students paid off:

For many the impact of that day was long lasting. Students asked for other books like Always Running. They interacted differently with me as a teacher because they had had a chance to interact with me outside the school building that for so many carried stigmas. Some students began to ask more questions and to grapple with the idea that their own lives were not foretold even if that was the message many of them had received year after year in their schooling. Students shared a positive experience with reading that countered the constraining experiences they previously held.

I can't claim that all the students were dramatically transformed or experienced widespread academic success as a result. These were students who had complicated lives and difficult experiences in school. I can say that they left that year having enjoyed and connected with a book and having experienced respect for their opinions about a book. While this might not sound revolutionary, for youths who face stigma and have difficulty engaging in classrooms, a positive experience with reading can open their eyes to more human ways of interacting with peers and teachers and begin to take hold of more positive scripts.

A group of adjudicated young people, students who had never read a book before, reading *Always Running* and embracing it as personally meaningful might seem an unrealistic goal. Yet Logan's careful planning and deep commitment to both her students and to the power of literature made this connection possible. We can help our students—all of our students—love literature as we do.

Grouping, privileging voice, encouraging exploration, discovery, curiosity, and taking risks—Logan combined all these elements to engage her students. But this experience also addresses another issue close to my heart—expectations. These invisible, urban students, when provided the opportunity, were not passive and decidedly engaged.

Although I have arranged many author conversations and interactions for my students—high school and college—no experience has surpassed what I observed and experienced that day. I was privileged to witness the power of literature as an observer, not a teacher. I was privileged to observe Logan's creativity, her ability to think outside the box to address educational equity for

> ■
>
> ***Children learn the*** *literacies of survival and education, regardless of class and race.*
>
> —R. Joseph Rodríguez, University of Texas-El Paso (July 27, 2014)

her students. I witnessed high school students totally immersed and engaged with a literary text and then with the author. I have had many unique and life-changing experiences in my teaching career; on that day, many seemingly divergent pathways melded into a unified and determined one—one anchored in the power of literature to move, to inspire, but also to teach, to be relevant, and to be monumental in the lives of our students—inside and outside the classroom. I carry these students, Logan Manning, and Luis Rodriguez with me every day.

As English majors, Logan and I read *Always Running* and were engaged and intensely curious; we appreciated the style in which Rodriguez conveys his message. We achieved identification, as Burke (1969) defines it. As English teachers, however, we consciously engaged with the novel in a different way, rereading it as our students might, creating learning and discussion environments conducive to encouraging students to read and experience it firsthand. Finally, we approached the novel as our students might. In our work, we must allow for our students' "So what?" "So, what do I get from reading these books, most of 'em by dead people?" Langer (2000) calls this "what counts as knowing":

> learning as being socially based, and cognition (in particular, ways of thinking) as growing out of those socially based experiences. Within social settings, children learn how different forms of knowledge "look like." As children learn to manipulate the tools of language to serve the functions and reach the ends they see around them, their ability to think and reason develops in a culturally appropriate way. . . . Learners' cognitive uses are selective, based upon the uses to which literacy is put within a community, and the learners' beliefs about "what counts" within that community. (1)

If we begin to think of the literature we teach from varied perspectives—as a passionate English major, an English teacher, and even, as Dewey and Freire describe, a co-learner, then, the way we create engagement pathways for reading literature changes. We see our students as an audience—distinctive yet multifaceted, filled with interests not necessarily ours—but just as curious, as adventuresome, always willing to take a risk. I have learned much and continue to learn much from them, particularly, when we explore the "so what" together.

To have a full competency in expression, images, stories, and words is power. This helps establish a personal authority that any member of a free society needs to contribute and positively impact that society. Imposed ignorance, bad schooling, or illiteracy gives that power to others. Poverty—which hampers the participation of persons as full, autonomous, creative, and adequately resourced beings—is also how one relinquishes power. Literature, rooted in books, although accessed by many means, is how stories and/or poems carry us toward such a world. It is therefore a revolutionary and healing necessity. Literature is one vital way dreams are realized. (Luis Rodriguez, author and activist, personal communication, January 21, 2015)

Blending the Canon with the New

5

If literature does anything, it broadens and deepens and enriches one's understanding of life on the planet—all the wonderful cultures, music, dances, experiences in abundance, literature, set the banquet, and it's up to us to decide how much we want to indulge. I went all the way, threw myself into the world and lived in literature and poetry as much as time would allow. It truly is a divine gift from the gods, and to experience literature on both ends, creating and receiving, will turn out to be our salvation; if anything serves to destroy oppression and injustice, it is literature.

—Jimmy Santiago Baca, writer, American Book Award, American Academy of Poets (personal communication, March 20, 2015)

■

"I came to see that the text alone is not enough," Hirsch said to me recently at his Charlottesville, Virginia, home. "The unspoken—that is, relevant background knowledge—is absolutely crucial in reading a text."

—Sol Stern, "E. D. Hirsch's Curriculum for Democracy: A Content-Rich Pedagogy Makes Better Citizens and Smarter Kids"

TOO MANY STUDENTS (even one is too many) do not readily connect what they read in our classes with how they communicate, think, write, read, listen, view things outside class. It's as if they see school-assigned reading as something separate from the rest of their lives, something kept in a silo apart from their real world. Without intrinsic motivation to read literature, students are far less likely to do so.

To address the issue of students' not reading the literature we assign, our profession has historically turned to punitive measures. I recently asked a colleague how classes were going. She said students were reading myths. I was overjoyed—I love mythology! But she continued: "And to make sure they are reading, they must take a three-question test; if they miss two questions, they must reread the story and retake the test. I told them it's best to read the story the first time." I made no response, but I felt for the students. If we rely on force to keep students reading, how can we hope that the literature they are compelled to read will ever be anything other than a burden, something for them to wall out of their personal lives, endure only until they have completed our classes?

Most students are not averse to reading, but they want what they read to be relevant. I call this the "so what?" factor: providing a clear reason and purpose. If we are only teaching to tests and assessments, we don't need rich literature. But if we want the literature we love to be both pleasurable and instructive, we must create clear crosswalks and road maps for our students. We must enable them to identify with each text. Blending canonical and contemporary texts helps our students make connections. By guiding them through discussion and collaboration, we enable and encourage their own discovery and exploration. By breaking the texts apart and experiencing the similarities and differences, they hone the literacy skills they need in their lives outside our classrooms: comprehending, decoding, inferring, surmising, reading, writing, speaking, listening, thinking critically, and creating.

The payoff of this approach is our students' clear understanding and belief that what we so love and want to teach them, our literature, lives beyond the walls of the English classroom. Literature does have a real purpose in their everyday lives. Literature can inform college, career, and daily tasks. Our students will be able to connect the dots themselves, not relegate literature to its own silo. When I spoke with Hal Holbrook, the consummate performer who to so many is Mark Twain/Samuel Clemens, about how literature speaks to readers on a purposeful, personal level generations after it has been written, he said:

> Huck Finn *is not a book about the word* nigger. *It's about racism, yours and mine, born of slavery as practiced in the American south. Trying to hide from the facts of it and the long arm of it pointing at us today endorses it. The word* nigger *is the most powerful word in* Huckleberry Finn, *it's the finger pointing at us and saying "What about you?" If you're afraid to face the word, ask yourself why? If it makes you uncomfortable, why?*
>
> *The word is not put in the book to save your feelings. It's put there to rouse them, to say, "Face it. This is you, too." We are not in Nazi Germany. Do we want to hide what we did, forget it? My people in New England brought the slaves from Africa in Yankee slave ships and sold them south. We did it. Face it.*
>
> *This book is not a cartoon like* Uncle Tom's Cabin. *It's told in the words of a boy living in a racist world with a drunken racist father, a boy who learns the value of a man with different color skin, a slave,*

and helps him escape. Huckleberry Finn has a long history of devious misinterpretations, from the Concord Public Library 130 years ago to the remark a Federal Express man just said to me, "Was Mark Twain a racist?"

*You can sell an opinion in our media world real easy. Substitute the historical word nigger with a nice modern one, **colored person**, and disown our share of racism. Struggling to understand it by not looking ourselves in the mirror and saying, "Could this be me?" Huck Finn is a mirror.* (actor, Emmy and Tony Award winner, August 28, 2014)

***Books of fiction** are supposed to spark the reader's imagination.*

—Joyce Cohen, personal assistant/manager to Hal Holbrook (August 28, 2014)

WHAT IS THE CANON?

The 1970s and '80s saw an upheaval among academics regarding the literary canon—its identity and its import in defining intellectual literacy—should teachers, particularly secondary teachers, continue to teach these works? In the late '80s and early '90s, two pivotal texts contextualized the debate: *The New Dictionary of Cultural Literacy: What American Needs to Know* (Hirsch 1988; 2002) and *The Western Canon: The Books and School of the Ages* (Bloom 1994). These two books stimulated energetic and passionate conversation among college and secondary teachers that resonates to this day.

We understand the canon to be a body of literature, including informational texts—Aristotle's *Poetics*, Plato's *Dialogues*, Henry James' prefaces to the twenty-six volumes of *The Novels and Tales of Henry James*, for example—that have "stood the test of time," a cliché that falls short of illustrative insight. Bloom (1994) provides a definition with which many professors and ELA teachers agree. Using Shakespeare as his metaphor, he extrapolates the traits that define canonical literature, its relevance, and its expansion:

> *[Shakespeare] is always ahead of you, conceptually and imagistically, whoever and whenever you are. He renders you anachronistic because he contains you; you cannot subsume him. You cannot illuminate him with a new doctrine, be it Marxism or Freudianism or Demanian linguistic skepticism. Instead, he will illuminate the doctrine, not by prefiguration but by postfiguration as it were. . . . One breaks into the Canon only by aesthetic strength, which is constituted primarily of an amalgam: mastery of figurative language, originality, cognitive power, knowledge, exuberance of diction. . . . Shakespeare will not make us better, and he will not make us worse, but he may teach us how to overhear ourselves when we talk to ourselves. . . . The Canon is indeed a gauge of vitality, a measurement that attempts to map the incommensurate.*
>
> *Subsequently, he may teach us how to accept change, in ourselves as in others, and perhaps even the final form of change. . . . [The Canon] is the image of the individual thinking, whether it be Socrates thinking through his own dying, or Hamlet contemplating that undiscovered country.* (40, 45, 51, 54).

Hirsch and Bloom each address the role the canon plays in our personal and collective memory. Hirsch's (1988) primary thesis is that a "cultural literacy" undergirds all successful reading and, concomitantly, a successful life. He establishes this focus in the introduction to the first edition:

> Although it is true that no two humans know exactly the same things, they often have a great deal of knowledge in common. To a large extent this common knowledge or collective memory allows people to communicate, to work together, and to live together. It forms the basis for communities, and if it is shared by enough people, it is a distinguishing characteristic of a national culture. The form and content of this common knowledge constitute one of the elements that makes each national culture unique. . . . This shared information is the foundation of our public discourse. . . . Cultural literacy is the context of what we say and read: it is part of what makes Americans American. (x–xi)

If we view our rationale and purpose for teaching literature as providing a bridge to literacy learning, we, too, subscribe to a "common knowledge" and believe that literature provides a viable and effective learning pathway.

IS THE CANON FOR EVERYONE?

I have had conversations with passionate, earnest ELA teachers who feel that some students, particularly those of color, living in poverty, or facing similar disadvantages are substantially challenged by a "traditional" ELA curriculum. They are reluctant to "plunge" these students into the canon, because they "know" that the students cannot negotiate the text, that such reading and literacy expectations are unfair and unrealistic. Hirsch disagrees, stating that "cultural literacy constitutes the only sure avenue of opportunity for disadvantaged children" (Stern 2009).

My response is similar to Hirsch's: as teachers, we should not avoid these texts or assume our disadvantaged students cannot meet the rigors of reading. Rather, like Carol Jago (2011), among others, I want students to stretch and grow and ignite furrowed-brow conversations: "Classroom texts should pose intellectual challenges for readers and invite them to stretch and grow. Reading demanding books makes students stronger readers and, over time, stronger people" (xvi). Our success lies in adjusting our approaches, strategies, and assignments for our twenty-first-century audience.

The canon is decidedly not reserved for the elite or chosen few, something Bloom wistfully laments in his "Elegiac Conclusion":

> What are now called "Departments of English" will be renamed departments of "Cultural Studies" where Batman comics, Mormon theme parks, television, movies, and rock will replace Chaucer, Shakespeare, Milton, Wordsworth, and Wallace Stevens. . . . You cannot teach someone to love great poetry if they

come to you without such love. . . . It is not "literature"
that needs to be redefined; if you cannot recognize
it when you read it, then no one can ever help you
to know it or love it better. . . . The strongest poetry is
cognitively and imaginatively too difficult to be read
deeply by more than a relatively few of any social
class, gender, race, or ethnic origin. . . . Even our elite
universities are supine before oncoming waves of
multiculturalists. (1994; 1002–15, 1019–20)

Bloom's comments limit the very possibilities and influence of the canon—its universality and power to speak beyond the ages and its ability to be a literacy resource as well as a source of pleasure. Bloom's position is antithetical to what we, as English teachers, work toward every day. Our goal is decidedly not to "protect" the canon as sacrosanct. Our goal is to help students love the canon as we do, not exclude them, even unwittingly. The canon is for everyone.

WHAT ARE THE "NEW" TEXTS?

Blending canonical texts with new voices, thereby using literature as a bridge to literacy, creates relevance and opportunities for personal identification for students. The new texts do not diminish the canonical texts; they enhance them, expand them, surround them with fresh air, for a very different and diverse audience. As poet Jimmy Santiago Baca says of the growth of rap and slam poetry, "Performance poetry didn't take anything from the page or from written poetry; if anything it found a new sibling or cousin" (personal communication, March 20, 2015).

While we consider how literature can open the world to our student readers, it may be helpful to consider how television—a much younger medium—has fallen short of its potential to educate its viewers:

When public television came onto the scene, the goal was to harness the power of television to educate and enlighten, rather than simply entertain. . . . Edward R. Murrow (1958) said, "This instrument can teach. It can illuminate . . . and it can even inspire." Many recognized at the time that entertainment was trumping inspiration and that there was a vast missed opportunity to use television to expand understanding, to allow viewers to see parts of the world that they may never see and to actively educate young and old.

—Neal Shapiro, President and CEO of WNET Thirteen, New York; former President of NBC News (December 2, 2014)

Tracing television's devolution can help us frame our work with literature: if we want texts to teach, illuminate, and even inspire, we must make them meaningful and engaging for our students.

Texts with a Range of Voices

ELA literature, K–12, now includes more women; more African American, Latino, Native American, and Asian voices; voices from around the world reflecting cultures, sexual and

> **Literature certainly has** *expanded my knowledge on other cultures and definitely other times.*
>
> —Student response on a reading survey

> **Literature isn't just** *the province of the college English major or the English teacher/professor. It is a window to life and relationships. If we are going to address that in the English classroom, we must move beyond simply reading the first five or ten chapters at a time of something irrelevant to our student population (whatever the age).*
>
> *I see the bridge as the device which connects what we read to how we live. If we cannot imbue that in our students, then I have serious doubts as to the efficacy of our teaching and certainly to the desire of students to become lifelong readers.*
>
> —Patricia Jones, ELA teacher
> (January 8, 2015)

gender preferences, religions, and difficult topics, challenges, and questions. Growing and stretching with their students and responding to different student audiences from year to year, many ELA teachers are ahead of the game. What they began in the mid-1970s and continue to advance is the nullification of either/or: the canon alone, with its richness and depth and wealth of past knowledge, or only new voices. Instead, ELA teachers have created a protean, side-by-side, integrated blend.

Texts in a Range of Media

If we hope literature will truly become a part of our students' lives and be a fulcrum in twenty-first-century literacy, we must help students see how it relates to the texts they know best: digital media and visual arts.

For our students, texts are not limited to hardcovers and paperbacks. In classrooms today most students have at least one of the following: cell phone, laptop, e-reader, tablet. They read constantly—text messages, blogs, Facebook posts, email, tweets. They have created their own language in order to communicate—a kind of über-collaboration. They watch television online, in new ways, and rely on YouTube, Vimeo, Flickr, Dailymotion, Yahoo! Screen, MetaCafe, and Twitch. If we can tap into these modes of reading and communicating while relating literature to their here and now, we can allay their initial resistance and/or suspicion. The formula of Aristotle and the rhetoricians who followed him is still pertinent: audience (audience, audience!), purpose, and occasion. Our students are our audience, and we must take them into account. We must use and capitalize on their penchant for the visual, audial, and collaborative.

English teachers have always brought the available media into their classrooms—transparencies, music, primary sources, for example—to round out and inform the literature. I have happy memories of transporting works of art from the African American Museum of Dallas to schools in the trunk of my car so students could see period art created by people of color. When I was growing up in Houston, my parents would routinely take me to the Houston

Public Library, where I could check out books but also record albums and art. These media were a part of my life, so it was natural to include them in my teaching. We must also be mindful of the media that permeate our and our students' lives today and use them to support literacy learning.

In today's classrooms, transparencies, physical works of art, and only hardcover textbooks have all but vanished, but the range of texts persists. My iPad is loaded with artworks, primary documents (scanned originals of period newspapers and journals), images (Brady's Civil War photographs, Rosa Parks on the bus and being arrested, the WWII internment camps, a horrific wall of dirt rolling in on an Oklahoma plain), museum exhibits, virtual tours of artists' and writers' homes, and videos that place students in the moment of a historical event or dramatic performance (Edward R. Murrow reporting from a London Tube station during the Blitz, London's National Theatre Company performing *The Tragedy of King Lear* or *A Streetcar Named Desire*, the documentary *OT: Our Town* capturing students at Dominguez High School, in Compton, California, staging a production of Wilder's play), and books—primary and secondary.

> *The same critical* thinking skills can and must come into play in television viewing as in reading. And our educational support materials are designed to develop those skills. In our increasingly fragmented news environment, it is essential for young people to learn to ask questions. Is this fact or opinion? Does the program establish a point of view? Do you trust the source material? Does the program exaggerate reality or does it show just one side of a story? These are essential life skills that can be applied to the written word, the online world, or television.
>
> —Neal Shapiro, President and CEO of WNET Thirteen, New York; former President of NBC News (December 2, 2014)

Texts Tailored to What the Students in Front of Us Need

Think back to Belzer's (2002) study of five adult African American women who did not "crave to read" (discussed in Chapter 1). Belzer concludes that Mattie, Laura, Diane, Tamika, and Polly see no connection between the canonical texts they read in school (a disheartening and distancing experience) and the reading they now do as adults for entertainment and information (108–11). This critical reading gap might have been bridged and perhaps even avoided entirely if teachers had introduced these young readers to texts that felt relevant to them. What might their relationship with literature be like now had they experienced Logan Manning's (2001) instructional approach of using "the power of narrative to help students imagine different endings to their own stories"?

We should never enter a classroom presupposing what students know, should know, don't know, could never know. Although we may be, and often are, aware of students' class, ethnicity, socioeconomic status, or other traits, we cannot allow this awareness to interfere with or inhibit their exploration of a work in the canon, even one completely unfamiliar to them. Rather, we must use this awareness to inform how we interact with them and guide us as we choose new texts to help contextualize the canon. When we blend in contemporary texts students never imagined encountering in school, they react with curiosity, questions, and interest and are eager to explore them. New texts help us tap into their world as long as we keep an eye on our instructional objective—to trigger the curiosity and interest that will make students want to discover the text.

A Word About Images

Regardless of geographical region, type of ELA class, and gender, students keenly respond and resonate with images—both primary and secondary sources—an approach appealing to their predilection of the visual. For example, the images illustrated here—a Bill of Sale for Armsted, a toddler, and the Mayan Codex—elicit students' curiosity and enhance literary conversation when paired with the appropriate literary text (see Figures 5.1a and b). With the Bill of Sale, students read and vicariously experience the reality of selling a human being in perpetuity, as evidenced in the "receipt" of the transaction. With the Mayan Codex, students, who may never have thought of non-Western ancient civilizations as having a spoken or written language when they read oral mythologies, find this kind of image revealing and curious.

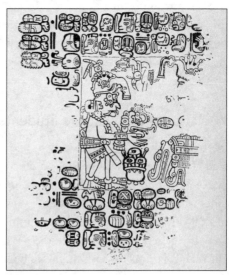

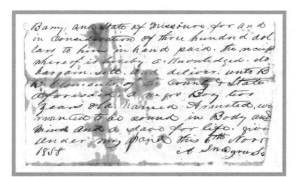

Figure 5.1a
Actual Bill of Sale for Armsted, a two-year-old child sold for $300 "to be a slave for life" on November 6, 1858, in the state of Missouri.

Figure 5.1b
This Mayan Codex gives students a glimpse into the culture of the first millennium A.D.

Blending new texts with the canon requires considering our goals carefully and reevaluating our relationships with texts. When choosing which texts to blend together, the following questions help me focus on my students' needs:

- Who are my students?
  - In what ways are they a unique audience with their own experiences?
  - What do they value?
  - To what topics, styles, ideas, or information sources do they gravitate?
- What types of texts do they read on their own?
- How do they interact with the texts and with me?
  - Individually?
  - Collaboratively?
  - How can the texts I choose help me give them more autonomy?
- What tools can I provide that they can use collaboratively and independently, with me and without me?
- How can I ensure that my objectives, while understood and clear, are also malleable enough to address immediate learning needs generated by guided exploration, discovery, and curiosity?
- How can I "get messy" with the text, whether new to me or one I've read many times before, learning and discovering along with my students?
- How I can prompt collaboration and reading outside class?

> *Opening a book,* whether in a digital format or in print, all of those forms involve language, cultures. And if we change, I think, our perception of words and how we use them, it can really open I think more doors so that parents, siblings, extended family members and teachers are all working together in that social transaction and network that equals literacies.
>
> —R. Joseph Rodríguez, University of Texas-El Paso (2015)

WHAT DOES PAIRING OR BLENDING TEXTS LOOK LIKE?

Once we are open to the variety of texts available, we can think about how to blend them in the classroom. Here are a few suggestions:

Tool 8:
Form for Selecting Texts to Pair or Blend, Appendix F

- Consider informational texts, poems, tales, mythology, plays, short stories, novels, letters, journals, interviews, speeches, films, social media, periodicals, music, videos, and artworks.
  - Maintain a journal in which you record possible resources as you discover them.
  - Ask yourself to what extent you think students will relate to and identify with each paired text. Completely? Mostly? Somewhat? Not very much?

- Identify aspects of texts that make them relevant for blending:
  - potential for comparisons and contrasts
  - applicability to contemporary events, people, culture, and so on
  - uniqueness
  - potential for student engagement.

Figure 5.2 is a form for capturing information as you select texts to pair or blend.

ASSIGNED TEXT(S)	THEME(S)	SELECTED TEXT(S)	GENRE	RATIONALE	STUDENT RESPONSE (After Reading)

Figure 5.2
Form for Selecting Texts to Pair or Blend

Below are some examples of pairings/blendings I've used with high school and college students. Each is a mixture of canonical and complementary texts—literature, documentaries, photographs, films, actual events, periodicals, informational texts. Rationales are included, as well as student responses. Each example focuses on a theme in the canonical texts that related to the complementary ones in some way. My goal is always to think of the students—my audience— and bring to bear the ideas and concepts that may resonate with them. (I've avoided some of the more obvious pairings and blends in favor of ones not so apparent.)

Theme: Civil Disobedience

Students understand the idea of Thoreau's focus on the importance and place of civil disobedience in America but are removed from the immediacy of his urgency and passion. This blend includes texts that are more relevant and immediate to students' present.

Canonical Texts

"Civil Disobedience"—Henry David Thoreau

The myths of Prometheus and Demeter

Complementary Texts

Speeches by Cesar Chavez: Cesar Chavez is a constant with me because I want a diversity of voices and ethnicities.

The Market Basket Grocery Chain Strike in New England (2013–2014): In late spring through the summer of 2014, two cousins, Arthur T. Demoulas and Arthur S. Demoulas, engaged in what evolved into an epic battle for ownership of a chain of family-owned grocery stores in New England. Artie T. was the champion of the common man—providing ownership shares for workers, giving back an overall 4 percent in 2014 to all shoppers because of the economy, working to maintain a family-owned business for the people. Arthur S. was the corporate cousin who brought in experts who were to revoke the 4 percent giveback, sell the business, and fire the employees—some of who had worked only at Market Basket for thirty or forty years. What happened next made the local, national, and international papers and news programs. Market Basket workers—including cashiers, butchers, managers, vendors, and builders—walked away from all MB stores. Only the people whom Arthur S. had hired remained, with no goods to sell. Customers boycotted and plastered their receipts from other stores on MB windows. Workers picketed and marched. Artie T. put up personal money to purchase his cousin's shares. This very present and immediate event is the quintessence of Thoreau's message. There are a plethora of resources, chronicling this "civil disobedience" event, including newspaper articles (*The Boston Globe*, *The New York Times*, *The Wall Street Journal*, *Huffington Post*, *USA Today*, BBC, *The Guardian* [UK], *The Daily Mail* [UK]), YouTube videos, clips from television newscasts, Facebook posts, and tweets).

"Ai Weiwei: According to What?"—Art Gallery of Ontario Exhibit, 2013: This art exhibit intrigues students every time I use it. Ai Weiwei's theme in the exhibit is civil disobedience: why, when, how, and consequences:

"A nation that has no music and no fairytales is a tragedy."

"Censorship is saying: 'I'm the one who says the last sentence. Whatever you say, the conclusion is mine' But the Internet is like a tree that is growing. The people will always have the last word—even if someone has a very weak, quiet voice. Such power will collapse because of a whisper."

(Ai Weiwei; both quotes appeared also in the exhibit.)

Black Lives Matter Demonstrations: As with the Market Basket protests, the Black Lives Matter meme has gone viral worldwide, with students and adults staging protests—all reported on and illustrated in newspapers, newscasts, YouTube videos, Facebook posts, and tweets.

Student Response

Choosing these texts, I looked for examples that linked Thoreau's ideas to today's world, and students have responded with a curiosity that has given them the energy and interest to study Thoreau intently. They are often intensely curious about the Ai Weiwei images as they relate to their assigned texts and are filled with questions built on Thoreau's message. They see and express the relevancy.

I first shared the Market Basket strike with students from Virginia, who were unaware of the chain or anything related to it. Their initial lack of awareness did not preclude their bringing their individual perspectives and questions. They were still able to relate to the situation.

Theme: Home

Home is a major and constantly recurring theme throughout literature, and many canonical texts fit within it. The ones listed here I have taught or been asked to teach. I adjust the complementary texts to fit each situation.

Canonical Texts
Grapes of Wrath—John Steinbeck
The Odyssey—Homer
The Scarlet Letter—Nathaniel Hawthorne

Complementary Texts
Percy Jackson and the Olympians series—Rick Riordan: YA fiction is important to a teenage audience, but this series also redacts canonical mythology for a twenty-first-century audience, much as J. K. Rowling did for legends.

OT: Our Town—a documentary of an adaptation of Wilder's *Our Town* staged by Catherine Borek's ELA class at Dominguez High School, Compton, California: This staging of Wilder's *Our Town* shows just how imaginative and inspired and frustrating and wonderful high school students can be. I love this documentary, and my rationale for its inclusion focuses on how wonderfully these young people and their teacher blow out of the water restrictions, hesitations, and concerns about urban youth, youth of color, poor youth, whatever label one wishes to apply, once and for all. Not easy by any reckoning, but Borek and her students accepted the challenge, and what emerges is a watchword for the effect great literature can have—it moves people to act, to reflect, to identify. These students begin to see and understand the differences and the similarities between themselves—their school, their community, and others' perceptions of them—and the characters in the play.

The comments at the conclusion of the documentary say it all. A parent says, "Well, I appreciate the fact that we saw a part of Compton that really does exist. We seldom hear about Compton being a normal community that has the same types of problems and issues as other communities." A grandmother says, "I know one thing; it is real." Some students who appeared in the play shout, "Our town is ghetto, I mean ghettoooooo," with huge smiles. Another student who was in the play says, "We broke down a lot of things people thought they knew about Compton. People are people. It really doesn't matter about race, background, or where you're from. We kind of made it a universal message. You know, people who live in Idaho can relate to us. We are not that different, but we are way different from what you think we are."

Homeless: The Motel Kids of Orange County—Alexandra Pelosi documentary; *The Dust Bowl*, featuring the letters of Caroline Boa Henderson—Ken Burns documentary; *An American Exodus*—Dorothea Lang: These two film documentaries and the photography/print documentary bring uniquely American events to visual immediacy as students read the Steinbeck and/or Homer texts. What is a home? What does that look like? What happens when one has no home, or when one loses a home, or when the elements simply—or not so simply—gust it away? Is a home a

A WORD ABOUT MUSEUMS AND EXHIBITS

Today, museums around the world are addressing the inability to "be there physically." A recent New York Times article (Lohr 2014), "Museums Morph Digitally: The Met and Other Museums Adapt to the Digital Age," provides a cogent and prescient analysis of what has happened and is happening in museums and why. Paola Antonelli, senior curator of architecture and design for the Museum of Modern Art, expresses the necessity succinctly:

We live not in the digital, not in the physical, but in the kind of minestrone that our mind makes of the two. . . . Museums have an important role to play in helping people explore and understand the emerging hybrid culture. It's this strange moment of change . . . and digital space is increasingly another space we live in.

Today, museums are immersive, interactive, and available on our tablets and smartphones. We can "bring" the museum to our students. John and I never go to a museum (or anywhere) without a camera. We have listed museum exhibits we think are not only good pairings but also ones we feel can pique students' curiosity and spark their imagination.

building? Is it large, small? Does everyone have a home? These video texts enable students to experience the assigned texts in fresh, engaging ways.

Home—Toni Morrison: This novel provides multilayered perspectives of home, the Korean War, posttraumatic stress syndrome, and the sense of place, while at the same time, feeling *out of place*. This thin novel is packed with action and images that only Morrison can deliver. Voices and ages are also multilayered.

Theme—Identity

Like home, identity is a pervasive theme. The challenge with such a recurring theme students see often is to make it appear not only different but more important, relevant.

Canonical Texts

The Scarlet Letter—Nathaniel Hawthorne

The Adventure of Tom Sawyer—Mark Twain

Adventures of Huckleberry Finn—Mark Twain

Complementary Texts

"Ain't I a Woman?"—Sojourner Truth: Truth's speech always connects with students. They are often unaware of the women's movement in Europe and the United States. That Truth is a voiced and assertive woman of color, not another Phillis Wheatley or Anne Bradstreet, provides a different perspective on the voice of women on the lecture circuit in the nineteenth century. How hard it must have been for her to stand before audience after audience, telling her narrative in her own voice and commanding their attention, especially as a former slave.

"Barbie Q"—Sandra Cisneros: Cisneros' "Barbie Q" provides a definition and exploration of identity via the iconic Barbie doll. The assigned texts are serious and textured; this short story carries a serious theme of identity contextualized in a deceptively simple plot that is not so simple.

The Absolutely True Diary of a Part-Time Indian—Sherman Alexie: Using the journey metaphor, Alexie takes readers on Arnold Spirit Jr.'s identity journey—one that includes self-doubt, angst, bullying, challenges—contextualized within the frame of race and racism. Regardless of ethnicity, gender, region, culture, and other codifications, students resonate with this reinvigorated coming-of-age text, for every high school student seeks and works hard to chisel out her or his own identity.

"A Room of One's Own," excerpt on Shakespeare's imaginary sister, Judith—Virginia Woolf: Woolf is generally the purview of senior English teachers. But there is a section in the book about identity that resonates: "What if Shakespeare had a sister?" Over the years, I have been surprised, wonderfully surprised, that young ladies and men both want to explore gender and the socially "assigned" roles. Recently, I have seen an uptick in this interest, particularly among young ladies. They are curious about the role of women and girls in assigned literary texts. This excerpt illustrates that their curiosity is not new.

"Maya: Hidden Worlds Revealed"—Boston Museum of Science Exhibit, 2015: This large exhibit includes diverse artifacts from a variety of aspects of Maya life. It captures how a culture defines and etches its identity in art, artifacts, images, architecture, utensils, games, religion, food, and text. Students who will never physically see this exhibit can experience the images and relate them to the assigned texts.

Unbroken—Laura Hillenbrand (book and film): This 2010 book, by Laura Hillenbrand, filmed in 2014, chronicles the experiences of Louie Zamperini, once a juvenile delinquent, who became an Olympic runner. Zamperini later distinguished himself as an Army hero. After a horrific crash over the Pacific during WW II, Zamperini not only survives starvation, lack of water, and exposure, he confronts the challenge of imprisonment and torture after capture. Themes of identity, resilience, refusal to yield, and human dignity resonate in both texts.

American Sniper: The Autobiography of the Most Lethal Sniper in U.S. Military History—Chris Kyle (book and film): This 2013 autobiography, by Chris Kyle, filmed in 2014, chronicles the training and experiences of Kyle as a master sniper who fought in the Iraq War. Kyle explores and describes personal, emotional, professional, and ethical challenges he confronted.

Always Running: La Vida Loca: Gang Days in L.A.—Luis J. Rodriguez: Written in 1994, this personal narrative (and cautionary tale) allows young readers to experience how Rodriguez found and fought for his identity.

> ■
>
> ***Perhaps I'm naïve,*** *but I'd like to think that film adaptations will turn out to help those of us who are trying to preserve the book as a unique intellectual experience. Nobody has ever made a good movie version of* The Great Gatsby *or* Adventures of Huckleberry Finn *because no movie can capture the experience of hearing a narrative voice on the page. The movie version of* Catch-22 *is a brilliant piece of filmmaking, but it cannot deliver Yossarian's final epiphany because it can't convey what's happening inside his head. Literature is a literacy bridge in the sense that it offers a connection between one person (a reader) and another (a writer), a connection that spans genders, races, historical eras, nationalities, and religions.*
>
> —W. Edward Blain, ELA teacher
> (November 10, 2015)

Student Response

Response to Sojourner Truth's speech is phenomenal. Many students have never read it, and they want to know more about her and her story. We then compare and contrast it with the assigned texts, and they have many thoughts on Truth and Hester Prynne.

The museum exhibit also resonates. The reticence one might assume students would have isn't there, despite class, ethnicity, geographic location. Their curiosity transcends any preconceived notions they may have had. Many questions arise not only about the exhibit but also about the assigned texts.

I keep returning to Woolf because female students have many questions about how authors render women. I want them to realize these issues/questions are not new.

The films listed are quite new; yet, many students have seen them and are more than willing to discuss them in an identity context.

HOW DO BLENDED TEXTS WORK TOGETHER?

The art of blending texts begins with finding them. One hard-and-fast rule I have is that I reread (or rewatch or review) whatever I am teaching in its entirety before I work on it with students. I am constantly collecting ideas. When the Market Basket strike was happening, Thoreau's "Civil Disobedience" occurred to me, and I began collecting newspaper articles, images, YouTube videos. Even if I do not know immediately how I might use content, if I think I might, I collect and file the material.

As students and I begin working together, establishing some version of collaborative learning communities (CLCs; discussed in Chapter 2) facilitates discussions and the formation of thoughts and ideas. Everyone reads the assigned texts, but not everyone reads all the complementary texts. I may assign particular readings to particular CLCs or let the CLCs choose the complementary texts that interest them. Sometimes excerpts of longer works are preferable—much depends on the students, the task, and time. That said, even when I first began blending texts, I didn't require everyone to read every book or article. Deep understanding through collaboration and sharing was my ultimate goal. I wanted students to share among themselves and with me what each had discovered, what each thought. My hope and aim was cross-pollination—for student A to decide she or he had to read what student B had read and so on.

My monitoring approach is to encourage collaboration, support independent thinking, ask guiding questions when groups appear stuck. I continue circulating among the groups, prompting students to express their thoughts, and refraining from providing answers. Ultimately, the groups should be an amalgam of collaborative, independent, whole-class participation.

Tool 9:
What Do You Think?

GIVING STUDENTS TOOLS TO CONSIDER TEXTS' RELEVANCE

Rereading and rethinking texts as we teach them, broadening the scope of the canon to include new voices, and articulating a clear, objective rationale are major aspects of using literature as a literacy bridge for our students. The final and most important aspect lies with our students.

To encourage and develop students' curiosity and predilection for reading assigned texts, we have created a series of guiding questions, What Do You Think? (WDYT). This instructional tool allows students to privilege their own voices and ideas, while also relying on their teachers' knowledge, guidance, and facilitation. This immersive, active process differs sharply from more traditional, passive methods, such as memorizing for the test, drills, and fill-in-the-blank exercises. The more we must wrestle and review and revisit a thing, the more familiar we become with it and the more we retain. This learning tool functions the same way. With WDYT, students necessarily compare, contrast, evaluate, analyze, distinguish, enumerate, classify, and synthesize the literary text and their relationship with it.

For most adolescents, self-absorption is a chronic fact of life based in developmental changes. In an age of screens, students bow their heads over smartphones and tablets. How do educators inspire them to look up, see the world around them, and find their place in it? By asking them to dive into literature.

> ■
>
> **Make sure your** students are encouraged to argue and debate these narratives; just swallowing them is unhelpful.
>
> —Toni Morrison, author (in my Twain, Faulkner, Morrison class, 2001)

Hard skills, such as fluently reading aloud, elegantly using parallel structure, or properly citing textual evidence, are vital to developing literate youth. However, true literacy requires empathy: placing oneself in a new context and understanding a contrary viewpoint. Literature, and in particular literature that addresses issues of gender, class, and race, provides students with a bridge to literacy skills and life skills. (Holly E. Parker, Coordinator for Academic Innovations, University of New England; ELA teacher; personal communication, January 14, 2015)

WDYT comprises three basic elements:

Between the Lines: Challenge students to interpolate and analyze what they are reading, using questions such as the following.

- What decisions do you notice the author has made regarding words, style, and story arcs?
- Why do you think he or she has made those decisions?

Who, What, Where: Encourage students to explore characters and situations, and then allow students to select characters and situations in the world around them that reflect the themes in the works they are studying. Ask them:

- Who is doing something similar or opposite and why?
- How has the world changed in terms of the situations studied in the works? Why are things different now?

Reflections: Help students synthesize their who, what, where analysis. Have them reflect on the following questions.

- What do the selected works mean to you?
- Do they relate to your life? If so, how?

- Do you see similar issues in your lives as those faced by the characters in the works?
- What do we know today that would have changed the outcome of events depicted in the work being studied?
- How would our knowledge of social studies and history, math, and science have changed the outcome in the text?

These questions can be used in independent writing and in CLC discussions to help students compare texts, analyze ideas, and perspectives developed in a group of texts and find relevance in texts. The more often we help students engage with these questions as they read, the more likely they will be to consider these questions independently as they read texts and the world around them.

THE PATH AHEAD

To Bloom (1994) and those who subscribe to his notion that poetry (and by extension all canonical literature) is "cognitively and imaginatively too difficult to be read deeply by more than a relatively few of any social class, gender, race, or ethnic origin (535–36)," I say, not so. I reject this notion, as do the ELA teachers with whom I have the privilege to collaborate around the country. Contrary to Bloom's further assessment that the canon is dying because many are under the illusion that "less knowledge and less technical skill is required for either the production or the comprehension of imaginative literature (as we used to call it) than for the other arts" (542–44), more skill and more knowledge are required from us as ELA teachers to bring our students into a new era of using literature, beginning with the canon, as a lifelong bridge for literacy learning.

We reject the notion that the literature we teach is so fragile and so special that only the anointed may peer beyond the veil and understand. Our students deserve more than this dated description of what such great and monumental texts offer in the twenty-first century. The canon blended with new texts and methods of delivery can empower and allow students who will never see Greece, never hear and see the Royal Shakespeare Company perform *The Tragedy of King Lear*, never walk across the moors of *Wuthering Heights*, never ride next to Rosa Parks on a bus, or sail beyond the mists into Avalon, to travel beyond our classroom walls and understand and experience both the canonical texts and the new texts. Our students can transcend time, space, place, social class, gender, race, and ethnic origin.

This chapter has explored the efficacy of blending other kinds of texts with literary ones—written text, visual text, performance text, digital text. Efficacy is the operative word, for our ultimate goal lies with using what our students find familiar along with what we find familiar to create a literacy bridge whose foundation is literature—both canonical and new voices. Yet one could still assert that nothing replaces the impact of literature—specifically, imaginative fiction—and never will.

It is not just English teachers who hold the text as primary. When we asked master documentarian Ken Burns if he considered informational and documentary programming as primary sources in comparison to print texts, he answered, "No . . . mostly, it can prime the pump," although he made exceptions for "rare cases of superb artistic and literary film work, that can at their best transcend the word." Interestingly, the skills Burns defines as necessary for viewers to have in order to evaluate and analyze television programming—"attention, critical thinking, and skepticism"—parallel the skills ELA teachers hope to foment with their students as readers (November 10, 2014). It is not a replacement for text. So it is with this chapter: the texts we blend with canonical texts provide context, facilitate connections, enrich—never replace.

Reading . . . can open new doors to how you see the world as well as new opportunities. We can learn about different things in our world and learn about other people's worlds. Through literature, we can learn about people and how they lived.

—twelfth-grade student, West Coast

Literature provides me with information about other cultures, times, and challenges, but it also allows me to expand my literacy skills beyond the classroom. It's great.

—eleventh-grade student, West Coast

Literature has provided me knowledge about other cultures without having to travel to a certain place to learn about it. As I learn I also challenge myself to read more and finish the book. As I read I learn new words and begin to use them outside class.

—twelfth-grade student, East Coast

epilogue

As we come to the end to our shared journey of exploration and conversation, this moment actually marks our beginning together as ELA teachers, embracing and seeking new learning pathways for *all* of our students. Using the literature we love as our literacy bridge, it is our fervent desire and hope our students will take what they learn, experience, discover, analyze, and evaluate in our classes to inform their lives well beyond our classroom walls. With this, our own instructional objective in mind, it is altogether fitting this book concludes with the words of inspiration and comfort that Dr. Marian Wright Edelman shared during NCTE's 2014 convention:

I Care and Am Willing to Serve and Work to Protect All Children©

(Prayer by Marian Wright Edelman)

Lord I cannot preach like Martin Luther King, Jr. or turn a poetic phrase like Maya Angelou and Robert Frost *but I care and am willing to serve and stand with others to build a movement to protect all our children.*

I do not have Harriet Tubman's courage, or Eleanor Roosevelt's and Wilma Mankiller's political skills *but I care and am willing to serve and stand with others to save all our children.*

I cannot sing like Marian Anderson or Fannie Lou Hamer or organize like Ella Baker and Bayard Rustin *but I care and am willing to serve and stand up with others to build a powerful nonviolent movement to protect all our children.*

I am not holy like Archbishop Tutu, forgiving like President Mandela, or disciplined like Mahatma Gandhi *but I care and am willing to serve and stand with others to protect all our children.*

I am not brilliant like Dr. W. E. B. Du Bois or Elizabeth Cady Stanton, or as eloquent as Sojourner Truth and Booker T. Washington *but I care and am willing to serve and stand with others to protect all our children.*

I have not Mother Teresa's saintliness, The Dalai Lama's or Dorothy Day's love or Cesar Chavez's gentle tough spirit *but I care and am willing to serve and stand with others to save all our children.*

God it is not as easy as the 60's to frame an issue and forge a solution *but I care and am willing to serve and stand with others to protect all our children.*

My mind and body are not so swift as in youth and my energy comes in spurts *but I care and am willing to serve and stand with others to protect all our children.*

I'm so young nobody will listen I feel invisible and hopeless and I'm not sure what to say or do *but I care and am willing to serve and stand with my peers and adults to save myself and all our children.*

I can't see or hear well speak good English, stutter sometimes and get real scared, standing up before others *but I care and am willing to serve and lift my voice with others to save all our children.*

God, use me as You will to save Your and our children today and tomorrow and to build a nation and world where every child is valued and protected.

Appendix A

SURVEY FOR USING LITERATURE IN THE CONTEXT OF LITERACY INSTRUCTION

This *anonymous* and *voluntary* survey seeks your ideas, thoughts, and suggestions about the literature you read and its relevance and application to you as students in school and out in your world.

In today's society, literacy goes beyond reading and writing about a text in your classes. Literacy now involves reading and communicating with and from many perspectives. Literacy in the twenty-first century requires you to be able to understand varied points of view and know how to respond appropriately in verbal and written communication in a variety of situations. You practice this kind of literacy each time you text, tweet, blog, and speak to an audience—friends, parents, teachers, people in the community, employers.

The anonymity of this survey is important; we want your honest, unrestrained perspectives. That said, please reflect on and think about your responses.

Thank you for your contributions.

1. List some of the literature (fiction) you have read in class.

_____

_____

_____

_____

_____

2. List some of the nonfiction/informational texts you have read in class—essays, articles, journals, for example.

_____

_____

_____

_____

_____

3. Using 1–5 as a scale, with 1 being the lowest, how often do you read assigned texts in their entirety? _____

4. As a follow-up to question 3, briefly list reasons for not reading the entire text:

_____

_____

_____

_____

5. Using 1–5 as a scale, with 1 being the lowest, how often do you use guides, such as CliffsNotes, Bookrags, or others, that contain plot summaries, character lists, quotes, and major themes? _____

6. This question is a follow-up to question 5. How often do you use the guides in the following ways:

    a. I use guides along with reading the text, but I read the text in its entirety. _____

    b. I use guides along with the text; I do not always complete the text. _____

    c. Sometimes I use the guides instead of reading the text. _____

7. Do you use the reading skills and strategies learned in your English class for reading in other classes? _____

8. Do you use the skills and strategies you have learned in English *outside* school (at work, notes to friends, nonassigned reading, blogs, tweets, for example)? _____

9. Using 1–5 as a scale, with 1 being the lowest, do you think the literature you read in class helps you outside class? In other words, do you think of characters or events or situations from literature in your everyday life and experiences? _____

10. Take a few moments to describe your response above.

_____

_____

_____

_____

_____

11. Think about and list some of the reading skills and strategies you now routinely use when reading books that you also use, or could use, in other classes and outside school—audience, purpose, message, style, word choice, tone, for example.

_____

_____

_____

_____

_____

12. List the books and magazines you like to read _outside_ your English class, as well as outside other school courses.

_____

_____

_____

_____

_____

13. Finally, imagine you are talking to other students and teachers around the country _without any penalties._ Being objective and proactive, how would you respond to the following statement?

Literature provides me with information about other cultures, times, and challenges, but also it allows me to expand my literacy skills beyond the classroom.

_____

_____

_____

_____

_____

_____

_____

Appendix B

CLOSE READING AND ANALYSIS GUIDE

This form lets you record a range of close reading and analysis possibilities for any text. When sharing this tool with students, you may wish to include only sections pertinent to a particular work.

AUTHOR:
TEXT:
GENRE:

Rhetorical Context

Writers always target their message toward a specific audience for a specific occasion and purpose. Marc Antony, in his request to give Julius Caesar's funeral oration and in its delivery, establishes an ostensible occasion—the death of Caesar—but his real target occasion is Caesar's brutal murder by his friends and colleagues. His target audience is everyday Roman citizens, and his purpose is to enrage the citizens, refocus their attention from Caesar to the murderers, and persuade the crowd to act against the perpetrators. Audience, purpose, and occasion drive the choice of genre, organization, and style of fiction and nonfiction/informational texts.

Audience	
Occasion	
Purpose	

Fiction/Nonfiction Conventions

Fiction and nonfiction/informational writers rely on the same conventions, or methods, to construct their text. Identify literary conventions/modes and describe how the author uses them in the context of audience, purpose, and occasion.

Point of View Identify point of view, analyzing/evaluating its importance to the text and message.	
Plot (fiction) Identify plot and, if applicable, any subplots, analyzing/evaluating its importance to the text and message.	
Message (nonfiction/informational) Identify the message, analyzing/evaluating its importance to the text and message. Describe the message's movement and its effect on the audience.	
Geography/Setting Identify the aspects of the setting that seem to influence the work as a whole.	
Events Identify the key incidents (historical or otherwise), relevant events, and transitional moments that drive the message, analyzing/evaluating their importance to the text.	

Character Conflicts If applicable, identify characters (real or fictional) and conflicts, analyzing/evaluating their significance to the text and message.	
Dialogue If applicable, identify use of dialogue, analyzing/evaluating its importance to the text and message.	
Tone/Word Choice Identify tone, word choice, or sentence construction, analyzing/evaluating its importance to the text and message.	
Irony If applicable, identify irony, analyzing/evaluating its importance to the text and message.	
Verisimilitude (fiction) Evaluate/analyze how the setting, theme, plot, and characters contribute to establishing and maintaining the appearance, or semblance, of truth within a literary work.	
Theme Identify theme, analyzing/evaluating its importance to the text and message.	

Style

Fiction and nonfiction/informational texts rely on stylistic conventions to engage readers and their imagination and reason. No single text relies on all the elements listed below, but many of them employ interesting and sometimes curious combinations. (This section of the guide works best when students work collaboratively and make group presentations to the class for whole-class evaluation, analysis, and discussion.)

Description: detailed observation and recounting of facts in support of the claim—sound, taste, motion, taste, touch (Corbett 1998, 41–42).	
Definition: as simple as literally providing a definition or as developed as using data, quotations, and/or statistics to illustrate and support the development of the claim (Corbett 1998, 97).	
Example: illustrative story, historical event, etc. (Corbett 1998; 42, 131).	
Anecdote: a brief story about a real incident or person	
Analysis (in tandem with description): literary analysis, data and statistical analysis, historical and scientific research; students deconstruct, decode, evaluate, and synthesize information (Graff 2003, 106–23).	
Relationship: cause and effect, antecedent and consequence, contradictions; organizationally, students can argue from an effect back to a cause or begin with cause and argue the effect (Corbett 1998, 113).	
Comparison: analyze/evaluate two or more things, searching for similarities, differences, inferences, authority, or inferiority (Corbett 1998, 102–103).	

Testimony: both objective and subjective proof, including limited and controlled use of emotional and ethical appeals; types include authority, testimonials, statistics, maxims, and laws (Corbett 1998, 124–26).	
Rhetorical question: an apparent question posed for effect and emphasis, sparking curiosity in the audience; the surrounding text may suggest an answer, but the objective of the rhetorical question is to move the audience to further questioning and critical thinking, seemingly of its own volition.	
Relevance (verisimilitude is to fiction what relevance is to nonfic-tion/informational text): an article, biography, essay, diary, documentary should always aspire to relate to the target audience, immediate as well as future; Shakespeare, Aristotle, Mary Shelley, Martin Luther King, Jr., the Declaration of Independence, and the Declara-tion of Sentiments all attest to the importance of a text's relevance.	

Appendix C

CLOSE READING ANALYSIS EVALUATION RUBRIC

Use this rubric to observe, guide, and quantify students' strengths and weaknesses, focusing on literary analysis, writing, and research for each area (and combinations). When sharing it with students, you may wish to include only points that are pertinent to a specific assessment.

AUTHOR	TEXT	GENRE

Rhetorical Context

Writers always target their message toward a specific audience for a specific occasion and purpose. Marc Antony, in his request to give Julius Caesar's funeral oration and in its actual delivery, establishes an ostensible occasion—the death of Caesar—but his real target occasion is Caesar's brutal murder by his friends and colleagues. His target audience is everyday Roman citizens, and his purpose is to enrage the citizens, refocus their attention from Caesar to the murderers, and persuade the crowd to act against the perpetrators. Audience, purpose, and occasion drive the choice of genre, organization, and style of both fiction and nonfiction/informational texts.

	4	3	2	1
Audience Identify the target audience and provide examples from the text to illustrate your choice.	1. Clearly identified audience(s) 2. If applicable, noted exceptions to target audience 3. Several illustrative examples throughout text 4. Wide variety of example types	1. Clearly identified audience but perhaps not all iterations 2. If applicable, noted exceptions to target audience 3. Limited illustrative examples throughout text 4. Some variety of example types	1. Identified audience in general terms; lacking specificity; not all iterations identified 2. If applicable, identified no exceptions to target audience 3. Few illustrative examples, not necessarily throughout text 4. No variety of example types	1. Did not clearly identify audience; lacking specificity; no iterations identified 2. If applicable, no exceptions to target audience identified 3. Very limited (1–3) illustrative examples, not necessarily throughout text 4. No variety of example types

	4	3	2	1
Occasion Identify the occasion of the text and provide examples from the text to illustrate your choice.	1. Clearly identified occasion 2. If applicable, noted exceptions to occasion 3. Several illustrative examples throughout text 4. Wide variety of example types	1. Clearly identified occasion 2. If applicable, noted exceptions to occasion 3. Limited illustrative examples throughout text 4. Some variety of example types	1. General description of occasion but not clearly identified 2. If applicable, no exceptions to occasion noted 3. Limited illustrative examples throughout text 4. Limited variety of example types	1. Attempt to identify occasion 2. If applicable, no exceptions to occasion noted 3. 1–3 illustrative examples, not throughout text 4. Severely limited variety of example types, if any
Purpose Identify the purpose of the text and provide examples from the text to illustrate your choice.	1. Clearly and accurately identified purpose of text 2. Several illustrative examples throughout text 3. A variety of example types	1. Clearly and accurately identified purpose of text 2. A few illustrative examples throughout text 3. A few example types	1. General identification of purpose 2. Limited, even conflicting, illustrative examples throughout text 3. Almost no variety in example types	1. Inaccurately identified purpose 2. Few illustrative examples throughout text, perhaps incorrectly identified 3. No variety in example types

Conventions

Fiction and nonfiction/informational writers rely on many of the same conventions, or methods, to construct their texts. Identify literary conventions and describe how the author uses them in the context of audience, occasion, and purpose.

	4	3	2	1
Historical Perspective Connect the work to historical or contemporary events or movements.	1. Distinguishes, analyzes, synthesizes elements and patterns in historical periods that compare and contrast with the present 2. Uses knowledge of a past event or period to infer and thereby draw conclusions about a modern event or period	1. Chronicles the developmental relationship throughout time and space between patterns and contemporary events 2. When appropriate, identifies which factors contributed to social, scientific, and humanitarian changes over time	1. Makes linear connections between past events and modern issues 2. May see similarities and/or differences 3. Does not address the import of these connections or intervening developments	1. Does not see and therefore cannot make any connections between the past and the present

	4	3	2	1
Theme Identify theme, analyzing/evaluating its importance to the text and message.	1. Clearly identified primary theme 2. If applicable, identified secondary thematic threads 3. Evaluation of text's support and development of theme(s) 4. Coherent and accurate analysis of development of theme(s) throughout text 5. Illustrative examples to support evaluation and analysis	1. Clearly identified primary theme 2. If applicable, identified secondary thematic threads 3. Some evaluation of text's support and development of theme(s) 4. Coherent and accurate analysis of development of theme(s) throughout much of text 5. Inconsistent illustrative examples to support evaluation and analysis	1. Generally identified primary theme 2. Did not identify, if applicable, any secondary thematic threads 3. Limited, inconsistent evaluation of text's support and development of theme(s) 4. Attempted analysis of development of theme(s) throughout much of text 5. Limited and inconsistent illustrative examples to support evaluation and analysis	1. Generally identified primary theme 2. Did not identify, if applicable, any secondary thematic threads 3. Almost no evaluation of text's support and development of theme(s) 4. Little or no analysis of development of theme(s) 5. Severely limited and inconsistent illustrative examples to support evaluation and analysis
Point of View (POV) Identify POV, analyzing/evaluating its importance to the text and message.	1. Accurate identification of POV 2. If applicable, accurate identification of additional POVs 3. Excellent evaluation of text's support and development of POV(s) 4. Coherent and accurate analysis of development of POV(s) throughout text 5. Many illustrative examples to support evaluation and analysis	1. Accurate identification of POV 2. If applicable, accurate identification of additional POVs 3. Adequate evaluation of text's support and development of POV(s) 4. Analysis of development of POV(s) throughout text 5. Some illustrative examples to support evaluation and analysis	1. Inaccurate identification of POV 2. If applicable, less than accurate identification of additional POVs 3. Inconsistent evaluation of text's support and development of POV(s) 4. Less than coherent and accurate analysis of development of POV(s) in part of the text 5. A few illustrative examples to support evaluation and analysis	1. Incorrect identification of POV 2. If applicable, inaccurate identification of additional POVs 3. Limited and inaccurate evaluation of support and development of POV(s) 4. Inaccurate analysis of development of POV(s) 5. No illustrative examples to support evaluation and analysis
Plot or Message Identify the message, analyzing/evaluating its importance to the text and message. Describe the message's movement and its effect on the audience.	1. Identified the text's plot or message, using supporting evidence 2. Charted or described the plot's or message's movement—high points, stressed points, turning points, low points 3. Accurately and comprehensively described the plot's or message's impact on the audience	1. Identified the plot's or text's message, using supporting evidence 2. Charted or described the majority of the plot's message's movement—high points, stressed points, turning points, low points 3. Accurately described the plot's or message's impact on the audience	1. Identified to an extent, but not wholly, the text's plot or message, with limited supporting evidence 2. Charted or described some of the plot's message's movement—high points, stressed points, turning points, low points 3. Attempted to describe in general terms the plot's or message's impact on the audience	1. Identified in very limited fashion the text's plot or message, with little or no supporting evidence 2. Inconsistently charted or described the plot's or message's movement—high points, stressed points, turning points, low points 3. Limited attempt to describe in general terms the plot's or message's impact on the audience

May be photocopied for classroom use. © 2016 by Jocelyn A. Chadwick and John E. Grassie from *Teaching Literature in the Context of Literacy Instruction.* Portsmouth, NH: Heinemann.

	4	3	2	1
Geography/ Setting Identify the aspects of the setting that seem to influence the work as a whole.	1. Identified key incidents important to conveying message 2. Distinguished among types of incidents (historical, fictional, factual, for example) 3. Identified setting or geography and its role in conveying the message 4. Analyzed the significance of setting, geography, and/or events to conveying message	1. Identified key incidents important to conveying message 2. Distinguished among some types of incidents (historical, fictional, factual, for example) 3. Identified parts of the setting or geography and their role in conveying the message 4. Analyzed the significance of some of the setting, geography, and/or events to conveying message	1. Identified some key incidents important to conveying message 2. Distinguished few types of incidents (historical, fictional, factual, for example) 3. Identified limited parts of setting or geography and their role in conveying the message 4. Attempted to analyze the significance of some of the setting, geography, and/or events to conveying message	1. Identified few key incidents important to conveying message 2. Distinguished no types of incidents (historical, fictional, factual, for example) 3. Identified few or no parts of setting or geography and their role in conveying the message 4. Very limited attempt to analyze the significance of some of the setting, geography, and/ or events to conveying message
Events Identify the key incidents (historical or otherwise), relevant events, and transitional moments that drive the message, analyzing/ evaluating their importance to the text.	1. Identified specific events succinctly and correctly 2. Charted or described these events to understand the trajectory of the message 3. Accurately and comprehensively evaluated these events' importance to the message 4. Analyzed comprehensively the impact of these events on conveying message to audience	1. Identified specific events succinctly and correctly 2. Charted or described most of these events to understand the trajectory of the message 3. Accurately and comprehensively evaluated most of these events' importance to the message 4. Analyzed comprehensively the impact of these events on conveying message to audience	1. Identified specific events inconsistently 2. Charted or described some of these events to understand the trajectory of the message 3. Attempted to evaluate some of these events' importance to the message 4. Attempted to analyze the impact of these events on conveying message to audience	1. Identified few specific events 2. Charted or described few events to understand the trajectory of the message 3. Attempted to evaluate few of these events' importance to the message 4. Inconsistent attempt to analyze the impact of these events on conveying message to audience
Character/ Conflicts If applicable, identify the key characters (real or fictional) and conflicts, analyzing/evaluating their significance to the text and message.	1. Identified key characters and/ or conflicts important to conveying message 2. Distinguished among types of characters (historical, fictional, factual, for example) 3. Evaluated characters and/or conflicts important to conveying message 4. Analyzed the significance of characters and/or conflicts to conveying message	1. Identified key characters and/ or conflicts important to conveying message 2. Distinguished among most types of characters (historical, fictional, factual, for example) 3. Inconsistently evaluated characters and/or conflicts important to conveying message 4. Inconsistently analyzed the significance of characters and/or conflicts to conveying message	1. Identified some key characters and no conflicts important to conveying message 2. Distinguished among some types of characters (historical, fictional, factual, for example) 3. Attempted to evaluate characters and/or conflicts in the text important to conveying message 4. Attempted to analyze the significance of characters conveying message	1. Identified few key characters and no conflicts important to conveying message 2. Distinguished among few types of characters (historical, fictional, factual, for example) 3. Lacked evaluation of characters and/or conflicts in the text important to conveying message 4. Lacked analysis of significance of characters to conveying message

May be photocopied for classroom use. © 2016 by Jocelyn A. Chadwick and John E. Grassie from *Teaching Literature in the Context of Literacy Instruction*. Portsmouth, NH: Heinemann.

	4	3	2	1
Dialogue If applicable, identify use of dialogue, analyzing/evaluating its importance to the text and message.	1. Identified use of dialogue 2. If applicable, distinguished among types of dialogue 3. Evaluated dialogue and its importance in conveying message 4. Analyzed the significance of dialogue in conveying message	1. Inconsistently identified use of dialogue 2. If applicable, distinguished among some types of dialogue 3. Inconsistently evaluated dialogue and its importance in conveying message 4. Inconsistently analyzed the significance of dialogue and its importance in conveying message	1. Limited identification of dialogue 2. If applicable, distinguished among few types of dialogue 3. Limited evaluation of dialogue and its importance in conveying message 4. Limited analysis of the significance of dialogue in conveying message	1. Identified no use of dialogue 2. If applicable, distinguished among no types of dialogue 3. No evaluation of dialogue and its importance in conveying message 4. No analysis of the significance of dialogue in conveying message
Tone/Word Choice Identify word choice or sentence construction, analyzing/evaluating its importance to the text and message.	1. Identified word choice and/or sentence construction contributing to conveying message 2. Evaluated the effect of word choice and/or sentence construction on conveying message 3. Analyzed the impact of word choice and/or sentence construction on audience	1. Inconsistently identified word choice and/or sentence construction contributing to conveying message 2. Evaluated the effect of some word choice and/or sentence construction on conveying message 3. Inconsistently analyzed the impact of word choice and/or sentence construction on audience	1. Identified some word choices or sentence constructions (not both) contributing to conveying message 2. Limited valuation of the effect of word choice or sentence construction on conveying message 3. Limited analysis of the impact of word choice or sentence construction on audience	1. Identified few word choices or sentence constructions (not both) contributing to conveying message 2. No evaluation of the effect of word choice or sentence construction on conveying message 3. No analysis of impact of word choice or sentence construction on audience
Irony If applicable, identify irony, analyzing/evaluating its importance to the text and message.	1. Identified presence of irony 2. If applicable, distinguished among types of irony 3. Evaluated importance of irony in conveying message 4. Analyzed importance of irony in conveying message	1. Identified presence of irony 2. If applicable, distinguished among most types of irony 3. Inconsistently evaluated importance of irony in conveying message 4. Inconsistently analyzed importance of irony in conveying message	1. Inconsistently identified presence of irony 2. If applicable, distinguished a few types of irony 3. Evaluation of importance of irony in conveying message lacked cohesion and specificity 4. Analysis of importance of irony in conveying message lacked cohesion and specificity	1. No identification of irony 2. If applicable, no distinction among types of irony 3. No evaluation of irony's importance in conveying message 4. No analysis of irony's importance in conveying message

This rubric is based on my research and the following references: *Teaching for Comprehending and Fluency*, by Irene Fountas and Gay Su Pinnell (2006); *The Skillful Teacher*, by Jon Saphier and Robert Gower (2008); *Thinking Like a Historian: Rethinking History and Instruction*, by Nikki Mandell and Bobbie Malone (2008); *Understanding by Design*, by Grant Wiggins and Jay McTighe (2005); *Dimensions of Thinking: A Framework for Curriculum and Instruction*, by Robert Marzano, et al. (1988); *With Rigor for All: Meeting Common Core Standards for Reading Literature*, by Carol Jago (2011); *Remodeling Literacy and Learning Together: Paths to Standards Implementation*, by National Literacy Exchange (2014); *Genre Study*, by Irene Fountas and Gay Su Pinnell (2012); *Classical Rhetoric for the Modern Student*, by Edward P. J. Corbett (1998).

Appendix D

REREADING TEMPLATE

CATEGORIES	What do I, an avid reader/English major, think about this as I read for enjoyment?	What do I, an English teacher, see as an opportunity for instructional reading and teaching?	What would my student, _____, think of this?	Conclusions/ reflections that will shape my work with my students
Author/Text What do I already know about the text? Is the title interesting? Does it make me curious? How do I feel about the length of the book? What do I know about the author?				
Type of Literature What's the genre of this work? How might this genre be relevant to me?				
First Impressions What do I notice about dialect, cultural nuances, foreign language, or objectionable language? How does that affect my thoughts about this book? What do I notice about sentence lengths? What do I think of these characters? Do I see myself/my world in them? What effect does the initial scene have on me?				

CATEGORIES	What do I, an avid reader/English major, think about this as I read for enjoyment?	What do I, an English teacher, see as an opportunity for instructional reading and teaching?	What would my student, _____, think of this?	Conclusions/ reflections that will shape my work with my students
Reader Prerequisites What information or references must I have to read this text? Am I likely to research background information or references I don't immediately understand? Do I have a method for such referencing?				
Plot What's my opinion of the plot? (Simple? Too simple? Convoluted? Intriguing? Incomprehensible?) If there are several plots, how will that affect my reading? If the plot is not linear, how will that affect my reading?				
Characters Can I identify the protagonist(s) and antagonist(s), even if I don't know those terms? How does the number of characters affect my reading? Are characters' names difficult to pronounce, remember, or track? Do any other elements—architecture, places, artifacts—function like a character?				

May be photocopied for classroom use. © 2016 by Jocelyn A. Chadwick and John E. Grassie from *Teaching Literature in the Context of Literacy Instruction*. Portsmouth, NH: Heinemann.

CATEGORIES	What do I, an avid reader/English major, think about this as I read for enjoyment?	What do I, an English teacher, see as an opportunity for instructional reading and teaching?	What would my student, _____, think of this?	Conclusions/ reflections that will shape my work with my students
Setting Am I familiar with this setting? If not, will I research it to find out more about it? Do I have a method for such researching? Does this setting have any relevance to me? Is this setting real/realistic, fantastic, or historic? How will I connect with that kind of setting?				
Style Which of these do I recognize *and* understand when I see the following within the text? How will this affect my reading? Tone Figurative language Dialogue/verse Personal narrative Example Anecdote Testimony Description Definition Relationship Rhetorical question Mixture of genres (e.g., prose and poetry) Factual information Historical fiction				

CATEGORIES	What do I, an avid reader/English major, think about this as I read for enjoyment?	What do I, an English teacher, see as an opportunity for instructional reading and teaching?	What would my student, _____, think of this?	Conclusions/ reflections that will shape my work with my students
Mode of Narration Which of these do I recognize *and* understand within the text? How will this affect my reading? First-person Third-person Filtered narration Omniscient Omnipotent Omnipresent				
Theme Do I understand the theme literally? Do I understand the theme universally? Overall, do I see relevance in this theme to me?				

May be photocopied for classroom use. © 2016 by Jocelyn A. Chadwick and John E. Grassie from *Teaching Literature in the Context of Literacy Instruction*. Portsmouth, NH: Heinemann.

Appendix E

STUDENTS' LITERARY ANALYSIS RUBRIC

Having your own guide can be quite useful while and after you read a text. You may use this template as an aid as you read, discuss, take your own notes, and even prepare for research. The information you gather will help you independently and in collaboration. You may use direct quotes and page numbers.

Author/Text: Note here what you think about the title, your familiarity with the author, any first impressions.

Reflections: As you read the text, take notes on your impressions or thoughts.

Type of Literature/Genre

❑ Short story

❑ Novel

❑ Poem

❑ Myth

❑ Folktale

❑ Fable

❑ Allegory

❑ Drama

❑ Graphic

Do you think this genre best suits, or works well, for this piece of literature?

First Impressions

1. What do you notice about the language: dialect, cultural nuance, foreign language, objectionable language, technical or unfamiliar terms?

2. What words or places are unfamiliar to you?

3. Describe what you notice about the initial sentence.

4. List the names of the characters.

5. Describe your first reactions to the characters.

6. Describe your first impressions of the text.

Plot Analysis

1. Identify the conflicts:

   man vs. man: man vs. himself:

   man vs. society: man vs. nature:

2. List a few important moments/events leading to the climax, if applicable.

3. List a few important moments/events leading to the single effect, if applicable.

4. Identify the climax or single effect and explain why you think it is.

5. Identify any subplots.

6. Describe your overall thoughts, observations, and concerns about the plot and subplot(s), if applicable.

7. Do you see any connections between what happens in the text to you?

Poetry Analysis

1. Paraphrase (write in your own words) what the poem is about.

2. Describe the tone and rhythm of the poem.

3. List any images or phrases you especially like or dislike.

4. Do you see any connections between the message of the poem and yourself: theme, actions, character actions, feelings, etc.?

Poetry Form

1. Identify the form of poem:

   ❏ epic   ❏ lyric

   ❏ narrative   ❏ dramatic monologue

2. In your opinion, does the poet accomplish her or his objective by using her or his selected form? Explain.

Characters

1. Identify the protagonist(s) and antagonist(s) and explain why they qualify as such.

2. Do you see other elements used as characters: architecture, places, artifacts?

3. Which character(s) do you especially like or dislike? Explain why.

Setting

1. Describe the setting(s).

2. Does geography play a role in the text? If so, how?

3. Is the setting familiar or unfamiliar?

4. Is the setting real/fantastic/historic? How?

5. Does the setting play a role in the text? If so, how?

Style: Review the elements below and comment on each as you see it exemplified in the text. Consider when the author uses each of these elements and the effect it has on you, the reader—for example, how does the author's use of description help you understand his or her main points or theme? How do the relationships in the work (and your relationship with the author) affect your views of the characters and the work as a whole? You also may want to list page numbers or cite brief quotations.

1. Tone

2. Figurative language: metaphor, simile, oxymoron, paradox, irony, repetition, personification, metonymy, hyperbole, synecdoche, anaphora, apostrophe, assonance, consonance, alliteration, onomatopoeia, anthimeria, chiasmus, ekphrasis (i.e., "Ode on a Grecian Urn" or Hawthorne's A), for example.

3. Dialogue/verse

4. Personal narrative

5. Example

6. Anecdote

Style (*continued*)

7. Testimony

8. Description

9. Definition

10. Relationship

11. Rhetorical question

12. Mixture of genres (e.g., prose and poetry)

13. Factual information

14. Historical fiction

Mode of Narration: Identify the point of view. Every text has a narrator. However, we may or may not like the narrator. We may not agree with the author's choice of narrator: for example, you may be a reader who prefers the first-person approach instead of an all-knowing, omniscient, narrator. Explore the following:

- Who is the narrator?

- How does the narrator tell the narrative?

- Do you like this narrative approach?

- What do you like about the narrator and the approach?

- What do you not like about the narrator and the approach?

- What would you suggest to the author about the narrator and the approach if you could make recommendations?

Mode of Narration (*continued*)

1. Identify the mode of narration (check all that apply):

   ❏ first-person   ❏ third-person

   ❏ filtered narration   ❏ omniscient

   ❏ omnipotent   ❏ omnipresent

2. What are your reactions to the mode of narration?

3. Describe any nuances or interesting elements about the way the author uses point of view.

4. What would you recommend or change about the narrator and approach, or why would you leave it as it is?

Theme

1. What is your understanding of the theme literally? Explain.

2. What is your understanding of the theme universally? Explain.

3. Do you see a connection or relevance to yourself in this text?

Conclusions/Reflections

1. Did anything surprise you in the text? Explain.

2. Did anything disappoint you about the text? Explain.

3. If you could speak with the author, what would you say about the text?

Appendix F

FORM FOR SELECTING TEXTS TO PAIR OR BLEND

ASSIGNED TEXT(S)	THEME(S)	SELECTED TEXT(S)	GENRE	RATIONALE	STUDENT RESPONSE (After Reading)

Appendix G

ESSENTIAL TEACHER RESOURCES

These websites, videos, and publications have been useful in our work and may be of use to you as you teach literature and literacy.

COMPREHENSIVE RESOURCES

The following websites offer information, ideas, and tools for (and often created by) teachers.

- Read, Write, Think (www.readwritethink.org)
  National Council of Teachers of English. Resources for teachers of English, including lesson plans, videos, and professional development.
- Edutopia (www.edutopia.org/)
  The George Lucas Educational Foundation. Articles and videos that address issues and ideas in education today.
- Literacy in Learning Exchange (www.literacyinlearningexchange.org/home)
  National Center for Literacy Education. Resources for teaching literacy in all subject areas.
- Teaching Channel (https://www.teachingchannel.org)
  Teacher-generated videos and teaching suggestions, as well as opportunities for collaboration via the Teaching Channel blog.

STATEMENTS OF PURPOSE AND POSITION

These texts can be helpful both in articulating our work and goals to others and in reconsidering and energizing our own work.

- www.ncte.org/positions/statements/onreading
  "On Reading, Learning to Read, and Effective Reading Instruction: An Overview of What We Know and How We Know It." National Council of Teachers of English (NCTE).
- www.theatlantic.com/national/archive/2013/06/how-reading-makes-us-more -human/277079/
  "How Reading Makes Us More Human." Article by Karen Swallow Prior in *The Atlantic*.

LITERATURE AND AUTHORS

The resources in the eclectic list below have deepened our understanding of texts and authors and allowed us to indulge our love of literature; they can also help students who are studying related topics.

- The Poetry Archive (https://poetryarchive.7dgtl.com/)
  Recordings (for purchase) of poetry read aloud, some by the poets themselves.
- Tell About the South (www.ageefilms.org/tats.html)
  Three feature-length films that tell the story of modern Southern literature.

The following texts are full-length documentaries about writers:

- http://vivascene.com/top-10-documentaries-about-writers/
  Includes documentaries on Plath, Nabokov, Rushdie, Duras, and others.
- http://documentaryaddict.com/about/literature
  Includes documentaries about Twain and Poe.
- https://m.youtube.com/playlist?list=PLYY7FdhF8Jbb-5DdwN_nq7frKb-jFOeS6
  A playlist of over seventy documentaries complied by YouTube user awritersruminations; includes many about authors whose works are part of the canon, such as Blake, Orwell, Austen, Bronte, and Frost.

TEACHING LITERATURE

These resources honor both what our students need and our own love of literature.

- The Great Books Foundation (www.greatbooks.org/)
  Resources for teaching canonical and contemporary works of literature.
- Conversations in Literature (www.learner.org/resources/series139.html)
  Annenberg Learner (Annenberg Foundation). A free video workshop for teachers of grades 6–12 led by researcher Judith Langer.
- *Speaking Volumes: How to Get Students Discussing Literature—and Much More*, by Barry Gilmore (Heinemann, 2006)
  A well-balanced and tested series of classroom strategies and recommended techniques for helping students approach literature in a clear and engaging way. The book features student activities, quotations, and prompts designed to facilitate student discussions on the meaning and relevance of assigned texts.
- "Literacy, Literature, and Learning for Life," by David J. Cooper (www.eduplace.com/rdg /res/literacy.html)
  A paper discussing a broadened concept of literacy, including (1) the implications of "real world" or more relevant literature in the curriculum, (2) the importance of focusing on

real-world themes when selecting and presenting texts in the classroom, (3) encouraging students to consider and identify a variety of resources (including multimedia) as part of expanding their understanding of literacy.

- *Transitions: From Literature to Literacy*, by Regie Routman (Heinemann, 1988)
  Discusses approaches for relying on literature as a primary element in developing students' writing and comprehension skills. Through detailed examples, Routman provides guidance on moving from standardized tests to literature to help students develop critical thinking, comprehension, writing, and expression skills.

- *Doing Literary Criticism: Helping Students Engage with Challenging Texts*, by Tim Gillespie (Stenhouse, 2010)
  Rather than providing examples of traditional literary criticism, Gillespie encourages and guides teachers in creating classroom discussions and activities in which students assume the role of critic to explore and understand assigned texts. The activities help develop students' abilities as critical readers and thinkers, while also expanding their skills and confidence in writing.

- "10 Ways to Teach Literature," *New York Times*, 2009 (https://www.nytimes.com/learning /issues_in_depth/10TeachingLiteratureIdeas.html)
  How to use the newspaper's archives when presenting major texts such as *The Odyssey*, the major plays of Shakespeare, *The Great Gatsby*, and *To Kill a Mockingbird*, among other literary works. Integrating these articles helps teachers present literature in the context of everyday issues and themes. The site provides links to multimedia and graphic elements that also help students recognize the relevance to today's world of the literary themes they are studying.

- *Teaching Literature to Adolescents*, second edition, by Richard Beach, Deborah Appleman, Bob Fecho, and Rob Simon (Routledge, 2010)
  Focuses on issues routinely faced by ELA teachers when presenting literature in secondary classrooms and provides innovative approaches to improving student interest and comprehension. Relying on classroom experiences, Beach and his coauthors guide teachers through developing multimedia, group discussions, and student-created activities that have proven successful in improving student performance and enjoyment of literature. A companion website features additional classroom resources and activities.

- Crash Course: Literature (https://m.youtube.com/playlist?list=PL8dPuuaLjXtOeEc9ME62z Tfqc0h6Pe8vb)
  Popular young adult author John Green's engaging videos about works of literature (*Romeo and Juliet*, *Things Fall Apart*, and *The Catcher in the Rye*, for example) spark students' interest while introducing them to larger ideas in the works.

TEACHING READING

- *Igniting a Passion for Reading: Successful Strategies for Building Lifetime Readers*, by Steven Layne (Stenhouse, 2009)
  A collection of strategies for helping teachers encourage student reading beyond the assigned texts. The goal is to help students regard literature as a lifetime resource, as a guide for exploring and understanding more of the world around them.
- *The Reading Zone: How to Help Kids Become Skilled, Passionate, Habitual, Critical Readers*, by Nancie Atwell (Scholastic, 2007)
  A guide for encouraging and developing successful reading workshops. The book takes teachers through strategies and evidence drawn from the author's success in helping students enjoy and better understand literature, while also developing their critical thinking skills.

LEARNING COMMUNITIES IN ACTION: LITERATURE CIRCLES, BOOK CLUBS, AND PLCS

- Literature Circles: Getting Started (www.readwritethink.org/classroom-resources/lesson -plans/literature-circles-getting-started-19.html)
  NCTE's readwritethink site introduces using literature circles, provides lesson plans, and correlates them to state standards.
- How to Create a Classroom Literature Circle (www.edutopia.org/literature-circles -classroom-book-discussion-how-to)
  Edutopia's guide to trying literature circles.
- *Literature Circles: Voice and Choice in Book Clubs and Reading Groups*, by Harvey Daniels (Stenhouse, 2002)
  A guide to help teachers implement literature circles in their classroom. Explores creating literature circles, encouraging and managing student-led discussions, and recommending companion literary and informational texts for students, all within the context of national standards for literacy education.
- *Mini-Lessons for Literature Circles*, by Harvey Daniels and Nancy Steineke (Heinemann, 2004)
  Builds on Daniels' earlier work on literature circles by focusing on recommended lessons and strategies for classroom management. Features examples of student activities, reading lists, and instructional strategies and approaches for making reading circles successful.
- *The Book Club Companion: Fostering Strategic Readers in the Secondary Classroom*, by Cindy O'Donnell-Allen (Heinemann, 2006)

Draws from contemporary research and the author's extensive experience in developing successful student reading clubs in secondary classrooms. The primary goal of reading clubs is to encourage student reading beyond the assigned texts and connect literature to students' understanding of the world outside the classroom. Provides resources for managing reading clubs, selected book lists arranged by grade level, discussion topics, and reproducible assignment sheets.

- How to Create a Professional Learning Community (www.edutopia.org/professional
-learning-communities-collaboration-how-to)
Just as a CLC gives students opportunities to learn together, a PLC gives teachers opportunities to grow in powerful and unexpected ways. This is Edutopia's guide to creating a professional learning community.

RESOURCES TO SHARE WITH PARENTS

These recommendations help parents support and extend their children's learning in your class.

- High School English Literature: Resources for Students, Teachers, and Parents
(www.findingdulcinea.com/guides/Education/High-School-Literature.pg_00.html)
Finding Dulcinea website. A comprehensive online guide to Internet sites featuring background resources for literary works and literature study guides. All sites have been reviewed for accuracy and relevant content. The site also includes information and recommended guides for parents to use while helping their children understand assigned texts, identify and discuss major themes, complete assignments, and explore additional recommended titles.
- Parent and Afterschool Resources (www.readwritethink.org/parent-afterschool
-resources/)
National Council of Teachers of English (NCTE). After-school activities and suggested books for students in grades K–12.

CONNECTING STUDENTS WITH AUTHORS

Putting students directly in contact with authors is a powerful way to engage them as readers, make texts meaningful for them, and help them see authors as people who have honed a craft that they themselves can also learn.

- www.slj.com/2009/08/programs/met-any-good-authors-lately/
This *School Library Journal* article, written by children's book author Kate Messner, is an introduction to hosting authors in your classroom via Skype.

- www.c-span.org/series/?inDepth
  C-SPAN2, Book TV in Depth. Videos of interviews in which authors answer questions that have been submitted by viewers.

The following links provide sources of interviews with writers.

- http://conversationswithwriters.blogspot.com/p/featured-writers.html
- http://therumpus.net/topics/conversations-with-writers-braver-than-me/
- www.theprooffairy.com/conversations-with-authors-podcast/

Below is a brief list of authors your students might contact. We've identified these authors because of the power of their work and their messages, but we encourage you to seek out the authors who speak to your students. Although writing letters to authors and hoping for a reply is still an option (and John fondly remembers his daughter's delight, years ago, when she received a reply from Judy Blume), you may also consider options such as Skype, conference calls, and Twitter or other social media.

- http://ellenhopkins.com/YoungAdult/
  Ellen Hopkins, author of fiction, poetry.
- www.booksbybrown.com
  Don Brown, author of historical fiction for young adult readers.
- www.marcaronson.com
  Marc Aronson, young adult fiction author who specializes in science-oriented themes.
- www.judyblume.com
  Judy Blume, popular author of young adult literature.
- www.sandracisneros.com
  Sandra Cisneros, author of *House on Mango Street* and many other titles.
- www.zakebrahim.com
  Zak Ebrahim, author of *I Am the Son of a Terrorist*.
- www.michaelkoryta.com
  Michael Koryta, author of *Those Who Wish Me Dead*.
- laughingatmynightmare.tumblr.com
  Shane Burcaw, author of *Laughing at My Nightmare*.
- www.emilyarnoldmccully.com
  Emily Arnold McCully, author of *The Woman Who Challenged Big Business—and Won!* (*The Story of Ida Tarbell*).
- www.tanyastone.com
  Tanya Lee, author of *Courage Has No Color: The True Story of the Triple Nickels, America's First Black Paratroopers*.

references

"10 Ways to Teach Literature." 2009. *New York Times*. https://www.nytimes.com/learning/issues_in_ depth/10TeachingLiteratureIdeas.html.

Abtahi, Laila. 2010. "Should Students Study with Spark Notes? Con." *The Mirador Online* (May 28). http://mhsmirador.com/opinion/2010/05/28/should-students-study-with-sparknotes-con/

Ai Weiwei. 2012a. "China's Censorship Can Never Defeat the Internet." *The Guardian* (April 15). www .theguardian.com/commentisfree/libertycentral/2012/apr/16/china-censorship-internet-freedom

———. 2012b. "Olympic Opening Ceremony: Ai Weiwei's Review." *The Guardian* (September 28). www.theguardian.com/sport/2012/jul/28/olympic-opening-ceremony-ai-weiwei-review

Anatole, Emily. 2013. "Generation Z: Rebels with a Cause." *Forbes* (May 28). www.forbes.com/sites /onmarketing/2013/05/28/generation-z-rebels-with-a-cause/

Applebee, Arthur N. 1984. *Contexts for Learning to Write: Studies of Secondary School Instruction.* Norwood, NJ: Ablex.

———. 1993. *Literature in the Secondary Schools: Studies of Curriculum and Instruction in the United States. NCTE Research Report. No. 25.* Urbana, IL: NCTE.

Atwell, Nancie. 2007. *The Reading Zone: How to Help Kids Become Skilled, Passionate, Habitual, Critical Readers.* New York: Scholastic.

Beach, Richard, Deborah Appleman, Bob Fecho, and Rob Simon. 2010. *Teaching Literature to Adolescents*, 2d ed. London: Routledge.

Bell, Phillip A., ed. 1865, 1867. *The Elevator: A Weekly Journal of Progress.* (May 5, 1865; June 27, 1867).

Bell, Sherri. 2004. "Transforming Seniors Who Don't Read into Graduates Who Do." *English Journal* 93 (May): 36.

Belzer, Alisa. 2002. "'I Don't Crave to Read': School Reading and Adulthood." *Journal of Adolescent and Adult Literacy* 46 (Oct): 104–13.

Berry, Ian, ed. 2009. *Tim Rollins and K.O.S.: A History.* Cambridge, MA: MIT Press.

Bloom, Harold. 1994. *The Western Canon: The Books and School of the Ages.* New York: Harcourt Brace & Company.

Burke, Kenneth. 1969. *A Rhetoric of Motives.* Berkeley, CA: University of California Press.

Chadwick, Jocelyn A. 2000. "Twain, Huck, and the Ministerial Alliance." *The Mark Twain Circular.* http://faculty.citadel.edu/leonard/aj00c.htm.

———. 2012. "Green Pens and Marginal Notes." *English Journal* 101 (May): 15–16. http://eric .ed.gov/?id=EJ998942.

———. 2015. *Common Core: Paradigmatic Shifts.* London: Cambridge Scholars Publishing.

College, Career, and Civic Life C3 Framework for Social Studies State Standards. http://www .socialstudies.org/c3.

¡Colorín *colorado!* 2015. "Video Interviews: Meet the Experts." R. Joseph Rodríguez. Last modified April 16. www.colorincolorado.org/multimedia/experts/video/rodriguez/.

Common Core State Standards Initiative. 2015a. www.corestandards.org/

———. 2015b. "English Language Arts Standards: Introduction—Key Design Consideration." www .corestandards.org/ELA-Literacy/introduction/key-design-consideration/

———. 2015c. "Key Shifts for English Language Arts." www.corestandards.org/other-resources/key-shifts-in-english-language-arts/

Cook, Caroline. 2010. "Should Students Study with Spark Notes? Pro." *The Mirador Online,* May 28. http://mhsmirador.com/opinion/2010/05/28/should-students-study-with-spark-notes-pro/

Cooper, David J. 1997. "Literacy, Literature, and Learning for Life." http://www.eduplace.com/rdg/res/literacy.html

Corbett, Edward P. J. and Robert J. Connors, eds. 1998. *Classical Rhetoric for the Modern Student,* 4th ed. Oxford University Press.

Cornish, Samuel E., and John B. Russwurm, eds. 1827. "To Our Patrons." *Freedom's Journal* (March 16): 1.

Crash Course. "Literature." https://m.youtube.com/playlist?list=PL8dPuuaLjXtOeEc9ME62zTfqc0h6Pe8vb.

Daniels, Harvey. 2002. *Literature Circles: Voice and Choice in Book Clubs and Reading Groups.* Portland, ME: Stenhouse.

Daniels, Harvey, and Nancy Steineke. 2004. *Mini-lessons for Literature Circles.* Portsmouth, NH: Heinemann.

Dewey, John. 1897. "My Pedagogic Creed." *School Journal* 54 (January): 77–80. http://dewey.pragmatism.org/creed.htm

———. 1916 [1997]. "Preparation, Unfolding, and Formal Discipline." In *Democracy and Education: An Introduction to the Philosophy of Education.* New York: Free Press.

Douglass, Frederick. 1847. "Our Paper and Its Prospects." *The North Star* (December 3).

———. 1859. *Douglass' Monthly* (January).

———. 1863. "Why Should a Colored Man Enlist?" *Douglass' Monthly* Vol. 4, No. 6 (April): 818.

Duke, Nell, Samantha Caughlan, Mary Juzwik, and Nicole Martin. 2011. *Reading and Writing Genre with Purpose in K–8 Classrooms.* Portsmouth, NH: Heinemann.

Eagleton, Terry. 2015. "The Slow Death of the University." *The Chronicle of Higher Education,* April 6. http://chronicle.com/article/The-Slow-Death-of-the/228991/

Emerson, Ralph Waldo. 1916. "Self-Reliance." In *Emerson's Essays: Selected Essays and Addresses,* edited by Eugene D. Holmes, 68. London: Macmillan.

Fountas, Irene, and Gay Su Pinnell. 2006. *Teaching for Comprehending and Fluency: Thinking, Talking, and Writing About Reading K–8.* Portsmouth, NH: Heinemann.

———. 2012. *Genre Study: Teaching with Fiction and Nonfiction Books.* Portsmouth, NH: Heinemann

Freire, Paulo. 1998. *Teachers as Cultural Workers: Letters to Those Who Dare to Teach.* Translated by Donaldo Macedo, Dale Koike, and Alexandre Oliveira. Boulder, CO: Westview Press.

———. 2000. "Chapter 2." In *Pedagogy of the Oppressed,* 169–70. London: Bloomsbury.

Gerwertz, Catherine. 2012. "Common Standards Ignite Debate over Student 'Prereading' Exercises." *Education Week* 31 (29) (April 25): 1, 22–23.

Ghansah, Rachel Kaadzi. 2015. "The Radical Vision of Toni Morrison." *The New York Times Magazine* (April 8). www.nytimes.com/2015/04/12/magazine/the-radical-vision-of-toni-morrison.html?src=xps.

Gillespie, Tim. 2010. *Doing Literary Criticism: Helping Students Engage with Challenging Texts.* Portland, ME: Stenhouse.

Gilmore, Barry. 2006. *Speaking Volumes: How to Get Students Discussing Literature—and Much More.* Portsmouth, NH: Heinemann.

Graff, Gerald. 2003. *Clueless in Academe: How Schooling Obscures the Life of the Mind.* New Haven: Yale University Press.

Grassie, John E., Exec. Producer. 1991. *Black Men: Uncertain Futures.* Interview (February). Maryland Public Television for PBS.

Herbert, George. 1633. "Easter Wings." In *Seventeenth Century Prose and Poetry,* 2d ed., edited by Alexander M. Witherspoon and Frank J. Warnke, 846. New York: Harcourt, 1982.

Hirsch, E. D., Jr. 1987. *Cultural Literacy: What Every American Needs to Know.* Boston: Houghton Mifflin.

Hirsch, E. D., Jr., Joseph F. Kett, and James Trefil. 2002. "Introduction to the First Edition." 1988. In *The New Dictionary of Cultural Literacy: What Every American Needs to Know.* Boston: Houghton Mifflin Harcourt.

Jago, Carol. 2011. "Creating a Context for the Study of Literature." In *With Rigor for All: Meeting Common Core Standards for Reading Literature.* Portsmouth, NH: Heinemann.

James, William. 1925. *Talks to Teachers on Psychology and to Students on Some of Life's Ideals.* New York: Henry Holt and Company.

Kids of Survival: The Art and Life of Tim Rollins + K.O.S. 1996. Producers: Dan Geller and Dayna Goldfine.

Kingston, Anne. 2014. "Get ready for Generation Z: They're Smarter Than Boomers, and Way More Ambitious Than the Millennials." *Maclean's* (July 15). http://www.macleans.ca/society/life/get-ready-for-generation-z/

Kinsella, Kate. 2014. "Cutting to the Common Core: Analyzing Informational Text." *MinneTESOL |Journal* (Fall). http://minnetesoljournal.org/spring-2014/cutting-to-the-common-core-analyzing-informational-text.

Langer, Judith. 2000. *Literary Understanding and Literature Instruction.* Report Series 2.11. Albany, New York: National Research Center on English Learning & Achievement.

———. 2001. "Literature as an Environment for Engaged Readers." In *Literacy and Motivation: Reading Engagement in Individuals and Groups,* edited by Ludo Verhoeven and Catherine Snow. Mahwah, NJ: Lawrence Erlbaum Associates.

Langer, Judith A. and Arthur N. Applebee. 1987. *How Writing Shapes Thinking: A Study of Teaching and Learning. NCTE Research Report No. 22.* Urbana, IL: National Council of Teachers of English.

Layne, Steven. 2009. *Igniting a Passion for Reading: Successful Strategies for Building Lifetime Readers.* Portland, ME: Stenhouse.

Lee, Felicia R. 2014. "Trying to Bring Baldwin's Complex Voice Back to the Classroom: James Baldwin, Born 90 Years Ago, Is Fading in Classrooms." *New York Times* (April 24). www.nytimes.com/2014/04/25/books/james-baldwin-born-90-years-ago-is-fading-in-classrooms.html?_r=0

Lemov, Doug. 2010. *Teach Like a Champion: 49 Techniques That Put Students on the Path to College, Grades K–12.* Jossey-Bass.

Levit, Alexandra. 2015. "Make Way for Generation Z. *New York Times* (March 28). www.nytimes.com/2015/03/29/jobs/make-way-for-generation-z.html?rref=collection%2Fcolumn%2Fbusiness-preoccupations&action=click&contentCollection=business&region=stream&module=stream_unit&contentPlacement=3&pgtype=collection

Lohr, Steve. 2014. "Museums Morph Digitally: The Met and Other Museums Adapt to the Digital Age." *New York Times* (October 23). www.nytimes.com/2014/10/26/arts/artsspecial/the-met-and-other-museums-adapt-to-the-digital-age.html

Mandell, Nikki, and Bobbie Malone. 2008. *Thinking Like a Historian: Rethinking History and Instruction.* Madison, WI: Wisconsin Historical Society Press

Marzano, Robert, et al. 1988. *Dimensions of Thinking: A Framework for Curriculum and Instruction.* Alexandria, VA: Association for Supervision and Curriculum Development.

Moeller, Victor J., and Marc V. Moeller. 2001. *Socratic Seminars and Literature Circles for Middle and High School English.* New York: Routledge.

Morrell, Ernest. 2008. *Critical Literacy and Urban Youth: Pedagogies of Access, Dissent, and Liberation.* New York: Routledge.

Morrell, Ernest, Rudy Dueñas, Veronica Garcia, and Jorge López. 2013. *Critical Media Pedagogy: Teaching for Achievement in City Schools.* New York: Teachers College Press.

Morrison, Toni. 2015. "I Know How to Write Forever" [with video]. *The New York Times Magazine* (April 8). Interview by Colin Archdeacon. www.nytimes.com/2015/04/12/magazine/the-radical-vision-of-toni-morrison.html?src=xps.

Murrow, Edward R. 1958. "Wires and Lights in a Box." Radio-Television News Directors Association convention, Chicago, October 15.

National Commission on Excellence in Education. 1983. "A Nation at Risk: The Imperative for Educational Reform." www2.ed.gov/pubs/NatAtRisk/title.html

National Council for the Social Studies. 2013. "The College, Career, and Civic Life (C3) Framework for Social Studies State Standards: Guidance for Enhancing the Rigor of K–12 Civics, Economics, Geography, and History." Silver Spring, MD: NCSS. www.socialstudies.org/system/files/c3/C3-Framework-for-Social-Studies.pdf

National Council of Teachers of English. 2013. "The NCTE Definition of 21st Century Literacies." http://www.ncte.org/positions/statements/21stcentdefinition.

National Literacy Exchange. 2014. *Remodeling Literacy and Learning Together: Paths to Standards Implementation.* www.literacyinlearningexchange.org/remodeling-together.

Next Generation Science Standards. http://www.nextgenscience.org.

Ocasio, Rafael. 2000. "Interview: Puerto Rican Literature." In *U.S. Latino Literature: A Critical Guide for Students and Teachers*, edited by Harold Augenbraum and Margarite Fernándaez Olmos, 145–52. Westport, CT: Greenwood Press.

O'Donnell-Allen, Cindy. 2006. *The Book Club Companion: Fostering Strategic Readers in the Secondary Classroom.* Portsmouth, NH: Heinemann.

Oxford English Dictionary. "Informational." www.oed.com

———. "Literacy." www.oed.com

———. "Nonfiction." www.oed.com

OT: Our Town: A Famous American Play in an Infamous American Town. 2003. Thornton Wilder. Director Scott Hamilton Kennedy. Film Movement.

Pinsky, Robert, trans. 1996. *The Inferno of Dante: A New Verse Translation.* Bilingual ed. Dante Alighieri. New York: Noonday.

Poe, Edgar Allan. 1846. "The Philosophy of Composition." In *The Complete Works of Edgar Allan Poe (Annotated with Biography).* Anaheim, CA: Golgatha Press.

Powell, Alvin. 2000. "Fight over Huck Finn Continues: Ed School Professor Wages Battle for Twain Classic." *The Harvard University Gazette* (September 28). http://news.harvard.edu/gazette/2000/09.28/huckfinn.html.

Rader, Hannelore B. 2000. "Information Literacy: A Literature Review." http://archive.learnhigher.ac.uk/resources/files/Information%20literacy/Information_Literacy-Literature-Review-std.pdf

———. 2002. "Information Literacy: A Selected Literature Review." *Library Trends* 51 (Fall): 144.

Raphelson, Samantha. 2014. "From GIs to Gen Z (Or Is It iGen?): How Generations Get Nicknames" (October 6). www.npr.org/2014/10/06/349316543/don-t-label-me-origins-of-generational-names-and-why-we-use-them

Reinhardt, Judge Stephen. "Opinion A: Assignment of and Failure to Remove Literary Works." *Monteiro v. The Tempe Union High School District.* October 19, 1998. http://caselaw.findlaw.com/us-9th-circuit/1281281.html.

Rollins, Tim. 1989. *Collaboration Tim Rollins + K.O.S.: Parkett 20.* New York: Distributed Art Publishers.

Routman, Regie. 1988. *Transitions: From Literature to Literacy.* Portsmouth, NH: Heinemann.

Saphier, Jon, Mary Ann Haley-Speca, and Robert Gower. 2008. *The Skillful Teacher: Building Your Teaching Skills.* Acton, MA: Research for Better Teaching.

Solochek, Jeffrey S., Cara Fitzpatrick, and Amy Sherman. 2013. "Politifact: Distortions on Common Core." *Tampa Bay Times* (October 13). http://www.tampabay.com/news/education/k12/politifact-rumors-blacken-common-core/2148256

Spencer, John. 2012. "Don't Bribe My Kids to Read." *The Phi Delta Kappan.* 94 (3): 72–73.

Stern, Sol. 2009. "E. D. Hirsch's Curriculum for Democracy: A Content-Rich Pedagogy Makes Better Citizens and Smarter Kids." *City Journal* (Autumn). http://www.city-journal.org/2009/19_4_hirsch.html.

Stotsky, Sandra. 1999. "Preface." In *Losing Our Language: How Multiculturalism Undermines Our Children's Ability to Read, Write, and Reason.* San Francisco: Encounter Books.

———. 2012. "Common Core Standards' Devastating Impact on Literary Study and Analytical Thinking." Issue Brief No. 3800 (December 11). www.heritage.org/research/reports/2012/12/questionable-quality-of-the-common-core-english-language-arts-standards

Tulgan, Bruce and RainmakerThinking, Inc. 2013. "Meet Generation Z: The Second Generation Within the Giant 'Millennial' Cohort" (November 6). http://rainmakerthinking.com/assets/uploads/2013/10/Gen-Z-Whitepaper.pdf

Twain, Mark. 1885. *Adventures of Huckleberry Finn: Tom Sawyer's Comrade.* New York: Charles L. Webster and Co.

———. *The Adventures of Tom Sawyer.* 1876. [1996] *The Oxford Mark Twain.* Edited by Shelley Fisher Fishkin. New York: Oxford.

———. 1900. "Disappearance of Literature." Address at the Nineteenth Century Club, at Sherry's New York, (November 20). In *Mark Twain Speeches* (August 19, 2006). Produced by David Widger. Project Gutenberg.

———. 1907 [2006]. "Interview." With Frederick Boyd Stevenson. "Mark Twain on the Scope of the Children's Theater." *Brooklyn Eagle* news special (November 24). In *Mark Twain: The Complete Interviews. Studies in American Literary Realism and Naturalism*, ed. Gary Scharnhorst, 647–699. Tuscaloosa, AL: University of Alabama Press.

U.S. Department of Education. 2000. "No Child Left Behind. Elementary and Secondary Education Act (ESEA)." www2.ed.gov/nclb/landing.jhtml.

Usher, Shaun. 2014. Compiled. *Letters of Note: An Eclectic Collection of Correspondence Deserving of an Audience.* San Francisco: Chronicle Books.

Wallop, Harry. 2014. "Gen Z, Gen Y, Baby Boomers—A Guide to the Generations." *The Telegraph* (July 31). www.telegraph.co.uk/news/features/11002767/Gen-Z-Gen-Y-baby-boomers-a-guide-to-the-generations.html

Wiggins, Grant, and Jay McTighe. 2005. *Understanding by Design*, 2d ed. Alexandria, VA: ASCD.
Woodruff, Betsy. 2012. "Goodbye, Liberal Arts?" *National Review Online* (December 13).
     www.nationalreview.com/article/335520/goodbye-liberal-arts-betsy-woodruff.

LITERATURE CITED

Achebe, Chinua. *Things Fall Apart.*
Alexie, Sherman. *The Absolutely True Diary of a Part-Time Indian.*
Allende, Isabel. *House of the Spirits.*
Anaya, Rudolfo. *Bless Me, Ultima.*
Aristotle. *Poetics.*
Barnard, Bryn. *Outbreak.*
Bell, Phillip A. *The Elevator.*
Bingham, Caleb. *Columbian Orator.*
———. "To Our Patrons."
———. "Why Should a Colored Man Enlist?"
Blake, William. *The Marriage of Heaven and Hell.*
Braithwaite, E. R. *To Sir, with Love.*
Brontë, Emily. *Wuthering Heights.*
Burns, Ken. *The Dust Bowl.*
Cisneros, Sandra. "Barbie Q."
Cofer, Judith Ortíz. "Quinceañera."
Cornish, Samuel E., and John B. Russwurm. *Freedom's Journal.*
Dante. *La Divina Commedia.*
"Declaration of Sentiments" from the first women's rights conference, in Seneca Falls, New York, July
     1848.
Defoe, Daniel. *Journal of the Plague Year.*
Douglass, Frederick. *Narrative of the Life of Frederick Douglass.*
———. "Our Paper and Its Prospects."
———. *What to the Slave Is the Fourth of July?*
Ellison, Ralph. *Invisible Man.*
Emerson, Ralph Waldo. "The American Scholar."
———. "Concord Hymn."
———. "Self-Reliance."
———. "The Snowstorm."
Faulkner, William. "A Rose for Emily."
———. *The Sound and Fury.*
Fitzgerald, F. Scott. *The Great Gatsby.*
Frank, Anne. *The Diary of a Young Girl.*
Frost, Robert. "The Road Not Taken."
Fuller: "Woman in the Nineteenth Century" (originally entitled "The Great Lawsuit. Man versus Men.
     Woman versus Women").
Garrison, William Lloyd. *The Liberator.*

Harper, Frances Ellen Watkins. *Iola Leroy, or Shadows Uplifted.*
Hawthorne, Nathaniel. "The Birthmark."
———. *The House of the Seven Gables.*
———. "My Kinsman, Major Molineux."
———. "Rappiccini's Daughter."
———. *The Scarlet Letter.*
———. *Tanglewood Tales.*
———. *A Wonder-Book for Girls and Boys.*
———. "Young Goodman Brown."
Heller, Joseph. *Catch-22.*
Hillenbrand, Laura. *Unbroken.*
Hinton, S. E. *The Outsiders.*
Homer. *The Odyssey.*
Hurston, Zora Neale. *Their Eyes Were Watching God.*
Irving, Washington. "The Legend of Sleepy Hollow."
———. "Rip Van Winkle."
Jacobs, Harriet Ann. *Incidents in the Life of a Slave Girl.*
James, Henry. *The Novels and Tales of Henry James.*
Keyes, Daniel. *Flowers for Algernon.*
Kyle, Chris. *American Sniper: The Autobiography of the Most Lethal Sniper in U.S. Military History.*
Lang, Dorothea. *An American Exodus.*
Melville, Herman. "Bartleby, the Scrivener."
———. *Billy Budd, Sailor.*
———. *Moby Dick; or, The Whale.*
Morrison, Toni. *Beloved.*
———. *Home.*
Pelosi, Alexandra. *Homeless: The Motel Kids of Orange County.*
Pepys, Samuel. *Diary.*
Plato. *Dialogues*
Poe, Edgar Allen. "The Bells."
———. "The Cask of Amontillado."
———. "The Fall of the House of Usher."
———. "Ligeia."
———. "The Masque of the Red Death."
———. "Philosophy of Composition."
———. "The Raven."
———. "Review of Hawthorne's Twice-Told Tales."
———. "The Tell-Tale Heart."
———. "To Helen."
Riordan, Rick. Olympians series.
Rodriguez, Luis J. *Always Running: La Vida Loca: Gang Days in L.A.*
Salinger, J. D. *The Catcher in the Rye.*
Shakespeare, William. *Henry IV.*
———. *Julius Caesar.*

———. *Romeo and Juliet.*

———. *The Tragedy of King Lear.*

Smith, Betty. *A Tree Grows in Brooklyn.*

Stanton, Elizabeth Cady. "Address to the New York State Legislature."

Steinbeck, John. *Grapes of Wrath.*

Sterne, Laurence. *The Life and Times of Tristram Shandy, Gentleman.*

Stowe, Harriet Beecher. *Uncle Tom's Cabin, or Life Among the Lowly.*

Tan, Amy. *Joy Luck Club.*

Thoreau, Henry David. "Civil Disobedience."

———. "Walden."

Truth, Sojourner. "Ain't I a Woman?"

Twain, Mark. *Adventures of Huckleberry Finn.*

———. *The Adventures of Tom Sawyer.*

Wilder, Thornton. *Our Town.*

Woolf, Virginia. "A Room of One's Own."

Wordsworth, William. "Preface to Lyrical Ballads."

index

Identifying with characters in literature
as English majors *vs.* English teachers, 77
as key to encouraging reading, 80
as stage in literacy development, 70–71, 73
Identity, as theme, 92–94
Images. *See* Visual tools/resources
Imagination, sparking through literature, viii, 2, 81, 85–86
Incidents in the Life of a Slave Girl (Jacobs), 50
Independent close reading, 56
Inference, exploring, 67
Information literacy, 45
"Information Literacy: A Literature Review" (Rader), 45
Informational texts. *See* Nonfiction/informational resources
Interactive vocabulary journals (IVJ), 29
Internet, role in literacy, 39, 89, 133

Jacobs, Harriet Ann, 50
Jago, Carol
on challenging students, 82
discussion of informational texts, 46
on exposing students to literature, 2, 15
Jones, Patricia, 83
Journal of the Plague Year (Defoe), 46

Kids of Survival (KOS) group, 23–27
Kids of Survival: The Art and Life of Tim Rollins + K.O.S. (documentary), 23–24
Knight, Teri, 12
Knowledge
appreciating different types of, 77
deficits, and need for literacy bridges, 43
prior, as bridge to literacy, 17–18
Kyle, Chris, 93

Lang, Dorothea, 91
Langer, Judith, 3–4, 64–65, 73
Learning. *See also* Collaborative Learning Communities (CLCs)
active, renewed interest in, 66
building on prior knowledge, 17–19
as component of literacy teaching, 16–17

and enabling/empower students, 14
and safe environments, 35, 64–65, 73, 75
from students, importance, 14, 17–19, 36, 53, 66–68, 77
Lemov, Doug, 43, 52
Letters of Note: An Eclectic Collection of Correspondence Deserving of an Audience (Usher), 49
Lewis, C. S., 16
Listening, and learning from students, 67
Literacy. *See also* Reading
and college and career readiness, 9–10
cultural literacy, 82
definitions of, 1–2, 11
and developing critical thinking, 2–3, 8–9, 36, 56–57, 85
and empathy, 34
importance, 1–2, 11, 97
information literacy, 45
as a process, 51, 72–74
and reading informational texts, 52–53
reading *vs.* visual literacy, 39
static/passive *vs.* protean/proactive approaches, 14
Literacy bridges. *See also* Canon, literary; English Language Arts (ELA) teaching/teachers; Expectations; Nonfiction/informational resources
building, examples, 2–3, 68, 70–77, 90–91, 94, 129–134
complementary texts and resources, 40–48, 51–55, 68
and the digital landscape, 13
incorporating diverse perspectives and media, 2–3, 8–9. 26, 50, 77, 83–85
and learning from students, 14, 17–18, 36, 53, 66–68, 77
strategies for engaging with literature, 68, 70–71
visuals and graphics, 28, 30, 37–39, 85–88, 90–91, 94, 130
Literal reading, 73
Literature. *See also* Canon, literary; Literacy bridges; Reading
communicating relevance of, 12, 15–16, 27, 38, 60–61, 68, 70–71, 85–86